THE
FLAMBOYANT
GARDEN

Also by Elisabeth Sheldon

A Proper Garden

THE FLAMBOYANT GARDEN

ELISABETH SHELDON

Photography by Dency Kane

HENRY HOLT AND COMPANY

NEW YORK

Henry Holt and Company, Inc.
Publishers since 1866
115 West 18th Street
New York, New York 10011

Henry Holt® is a registered trademark of
Henry Holt and Company, Inc.

Published in Canada by Fitzhenry & Whiteside Ltd.,
195 Allstate Parkway, Markham, Ontario L3R 4T8.

Library of Congress Cataloging-in-Publication Data
Sheldon, Elisabeth.
The flamboyant garden / Elisabeth Sheldon. — 1st ed.
      p.   cm.
Includes bibliographical references and index.
1. Color in gardening. 2. Flowers—Color. 3. Gardens—Design.
I. Title.
SB454.3.C64S48   1997   96-16471
635.9'68—dc20   CIP

ISBN 0-8050-3798-5

Henry Holt books are available for special promotions and
premiums. For details contact: Director, Special Markets.

First Edition—1997

DESIGNED BY LUCY ALBANESE

Printed in the United States of America
All first editions are printed on acid-free paper. ∞

10 9 8 7 6 5 4 3 2 1

THIS ONE IS FOR GEORGE

CONTENTS

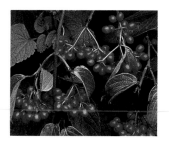

THE
FLAMBOYANT
GARDEN

INTRODUCTION

Perhaps I should say straightaway what I mean by "hot" colors—although many people will already know that orange, vermilion, scarlet, and strong yellows are called hot, while those on the opposite side of the color wheel—blue, green, lavender, gray—are called cool. Colors in the latter group are restful and soothing to the eye, while those in the first group stimulate the eye, the effect being exhilarating or irritating, even exhausting, depending on how they have been handled by the person who created the picture, fabric, interior, garden, or other composition in which they occur.

It seems to me that, until quite recently, Americans, British, Scandinavians, and all other northerners in the Western Hemisphere have been taught that Cool is Better, Cool is Classier, more refined. Do you remember memorizing in school

Robert Browning's "Home Thoughts from Abroad" ("Oh, to be in England, / now that April's there . . .")? In the last lines he praises the small, pale "buttercup, the little children's dower, / Far brighter than this gaudy melon flower." "Gaudy"—that was the damning word. I, for one, was impressed.

We gathered from many indications that we dare not look gaudy. That was all right for people on tropical islands but not for us northerners. Consequently, although the country and the climate in most of the United States are quite different from those of Britain, we took our tastes largely from the British. Naturally, since they were our founding fathers and mothers. For several hundred years we've adorned our bodies, our houses, and our gardens—those of us with "taste," that is—constrainedly and conservatively. We've worn the little black suit, gray flannels, and Scottish tweeds. Dresses of pale rose or blue, dark crimson, even, were acceptable, but not orange. No one with any claim to class would wear orange. Small children were dressed in white, blue, or pale pink, perhaps pale yellow. Jackets of schoolchildren were navy blue or brown.

Now a group of children being herded down the street looks like a flock of tropical birds. Times have changed, and with them our ideas of what is permissible in the use of color.

To what can we attribute the change? No doubt to the fact that we are in closer contact with people from all over the globe rather than almost exclusively with Europeans, as was formerly the case. We visit those tropical islands, as well as Asia and India, and people from those places come here. We have been first shocked, then delighted by their ways with food and fabrics. We admired and began to adopt their designs and color combinations.

Years ago we were taught that certain colors didn't "go" together. Red didn't go with yellow, for example (yet how many flowers have red petals and yellow centers?), nor orange with pink. But now we respond enthusiastically to Oriental fabrics that combine those colors.

And so in our gardens we have, as a rule, been desperately Nordic, imitating as best we could in our for the most part brutal climates the tenderly hued horticultural confections that are so appropriate to the misty isles of Britain.

Yet, as I say, our climate is quite different since in most parts of the country we have extremes of both cold and hot weather. Here in upstate New York, for example, we go from Vladivostok temperatures to those of central Africa, sometimes in quick succession. We should consider these extremes of temperature when we are planning our gardens.

We should also think about the part light has to play in the aspect of a garden. Penelope Hobhouse, British gardener and garden writer, says:

> The illumination of bright sunlight tends to faintly yellow all flower color; in countries with especially fierce midday sun, even intensely vivid flowers in scarlet or bright orange appear faded. For this reason, in tropical countries, the brightest colors are needed to satisfy the cravings for strong garden color. In a temperate climate, under gray skies, on the other hand, muted, low-toned green leaves glow more brilliantly, white and pastel-colored flowers shine, but the brightest hues become garish.[*]

Now I have spent many years orchestrating a long, undulating mixed border in ever-changing but always delicate Whistlerian compositions of gray and pale sulfur, of silver, rose and white, white and cerulean blue, lavender and lime—principally pastel, except for the occasional touch of crimson or purple. Utterly refined. I have loved this border with all my heart, and indeed I love it still. Yet I wanted something more. Even an Englishman can feel the need for strong color, for Christopher

[*]*Color in Your Garden* (Boston, Toronto: Little, Brown, 1985), p. 38.

*E*ast *end of the long mixed border in midsummer, when astilbe, lythrum, and veronicastrum predominate.*

Lloyd said, when defending his use of a brassy coreopsis (and admitting that it was a little "riotous"), "But then, we do not all want to float endlessly amongst silvers and greys."* I had thought that I did, but as the years passed I began to yearn for more stimulating stuff. Tea was all very well, but more and more I craved brandy. I began to try to work rudbeckias, heliopsis, and flaming 'Enchantment' lilies into my compositions, but without success; I just couldn't bring it off. The colors jarred and clashed, they jumped out ahead of their neighbors, they refused to harmonize,

*The Well-Tempered Garden (New York: Random House, 1985), p. 83.

to be part of a whole. So out they came and were banished to distant holding beds, where I visited them from time to time, surreptitiously, to peer down avidly into their fierce little faces and wish I could gather them all into a garden. A proper garden, where each of them would be a valuable member of society, where each would be a contributor to the total effect instead of being a troublemaker. I had become a closet lover of gaudy flowers.

But then I began to think of a way to come out. I knew very well that other gardeners had used hot colors successfully. The most often used solution has been to employ vivid colors sparingly, as occasional bursts of brilliance surrounded by masses of gray, white, or, at any rate, muted cool colors. In this way they've been used to contrast rather than to harmonize with other colors. One solution used by Gertrude Jekyll, the great turn-of-the-century English horticulturist, was to place the cool colors at either end of a long border, and, working gradually through a series of carefully planned gradations of color, to let them grow warmer and warmer, toward the center where they made a great conflagration. In this way she was able to use colors that harmonized with one another, rather than contrasted. It must have been sensational, and probably required only a thousand or so plants and a staff of twelve professional gardeners to maintain it. But those of us with modest means and little or no help must devise simpler solutions to our gardening problems.

As I cast about for a solution to mine, I thought of making a small garden in which I could use comparatively few plants. I decided to work on the system of combining colors that are closely related on the color wheel rather than those that are opposite one another. I aimed for a dazzling effect, certainly, but I wanted to produce it harmoniously. I thought that if I planted a chrome yellow heliopsis, say, next to an orange zinnia, next to a scarlet lychnis, next to a crimson dahlia, they would harmonize because they each shared a pigment with their neighbor. The heliopsis and the zinnia would share yellow, the zinnia and the lychnis would share orange, the lychnis and the dahlia, red. It should work, I thought.

I began to look for a site for the garden where it couldn't be seen from the long border. If I'd lived in a manor house, I'd no doubt have had old walls and hedges that would have enabled me to tuck my new garden away from the old one. Or if I'd had more eventful territory—that is, gardenable land on different levels—it could have been kept out of sight. As it was, I had a Victorian farmhouse with flat land all around it except for a ravine that ran quite close to the house on the north side—no place for a perennial garden there. The long border was on the south side of the house, and in the east was the woods garden. On the west side were barns that provided a background for roses and other shrubs. I finally selected a spot at the east end of the old perennial nursery adjacent to the woods garden. A grass path led to what had been rows of nursery plants but now was only a weed patch. Soon, I hoped, it would lead to something beautiful: a spectacular enclosed garden.

I suppose I should also admit to having always had a hankering for a secret garden. But doesn't everyone? Doesn't the undying popularity of Frances Hodgson Burnett's book attest to the fact? Psychologists would probably tell us that we all have a primal urge to be enclosed. I remember the joy of "making houses" indoors on rainy days when my mother would let us children construct them with the aid of blankets, tables, and chairs. And I remember we dug caves in the ground and built a house in a tree, complete with flimsy walls and roof. At any rate, I think that people may get a feeling of satisfaction when entering an enclosed garden that goes beyond that given by the garden's design and the plants growing in it. I sometimes go to sit in my garden on a sunny day in winter when it's filled with nothing but snow.

There were, however, more serious reasons for creating an enclosure. I wanted to segregate the new garden not only to keep the hot colors from interfering with the cool ones, but because of a theory I have—a theory about the wearing qualities of intense orange and scarlet. It seems to me that, while, on first encounter, these colors stimulate, even exhilarate the viewer, they will, if constantly in sight, end by wearying the eye and depressing the spirits. A double row of *Salvia splendens* lining the front walk must become almost unbearable after the initial high resulting from their installation wears off. I've compared this phenomenon of diminishing returns to that of a tenor's hitting high C. When this occurs as a climax to a glorious aria, it lifts us out of our seats, thrilled to the core. But if the high C is repeated over and over as it is (nine times) in that famous number from Donizetti's *The Daughter of the Regiment,* it makes us—some of us, anyway—want to scream. It's not just tiresome; it's really painful. Surely those high, wild utterances, whether of sound or color, should be reserved for special dramatic moments and not be allowed to become irritating and wearisome.

Operating on this principle, I determined to enclose my garden so that it could be viewed only deliberately. One could go and sit in it when one wanted a lift and leave when the desirable degree of intoxication had been reached.

Having the garden enclosed would also provide the element of surprise that is held in such high esteem by garden designers who write books. I thought with glee of visitors strolling the length of my refined pastel border, then turning the corner and opening the gate, when they would fall over backward, knocked flat by the flaming colors in my secret jungle. The impact would be all the more powerful as they would pass through part of the shady woods garden before entering the new garden, which is in full sun. Since it is enclosed by a high fence, I must admit that at midday in midsummer, it's hot in more ways than one. When you come out of it into the cool green shade, it's like jumping from a sauna into the sea.

DESIGNING THE GARDEN

hen considering ways to enclose the garden, I thought first of hedges. However, since the area is small (twenty by thirty feet), I decided they'd take up too much room, to say nothing of water and nourishment. And who was to clip them? Besides, I didn't have time to wait for them to grow. I settled for plain cedar fencing with redwood corner posts. The gate has a semicircular opening cut in the top, through which one can peek before entering, to lessen the shock.

The fence boards are five and a half feet tall and are set three-quarters of an inch apart to allow for the circulation of air. It is for that reason too that I had them set several inches above the ground, not having taken into account that it would also allow for the circulation of rabbits. I'm now planning to stretch chicken wire around the bottom of the fence on the outside.

A *path between the woods garden, on the left, and the heathers and shrubs at the east end of the east border. The path leads to the hot-color garden gate.*

My long border is designed informally, having at the back a low, straight stone wall that repeats the line of the house. The border swoops in and out, its depth ranging from four to thirty feet. It is two hundred fifty feet long but is held together—or so I hope—by the repetition of color, texture, and form. Although it billows about, it gives one (when it is weed-free and neatly edged, and the lawn has been mowed) a feeling of peace and serenity, notwithstanding its informality.

The new garden, though, needed a formal design, since it would be contained within a small, insistent rectangle. Swooping curves would not do here. I bisected it with a central walk, crossed by rectangles at either end and one (almost a square) in the center. I paved all these pedestrian areas with brick. Since I'd raised the planting area by adding manure and grit, I retained the soil, while defining the walkways, by sinking four-inch-wide cedar boards down behind the bricks, all the way around. So it's a simple, tight little design—no flights of fancy. I wanted to leave that to the plants.

Those who do not shudder at the idea, and who may be thinking of making an enclosed garden of hot-colored flowers, should think hard about the building materials they are to use. The background should enhance rather than interfere with the incendiary hues of the plants. A dark yew hedge would be wonderful, but a dark green painted fence could be disastrous. It's hard to find green in a can that doesn't fight with or cancel out natural greens. Choose carefully or maybe play it safe like me, and use cedar, which weathers to a good silvery gray. White fencing might provide even more drama. Above all things, avoid a background color that contains yellow, red, or brown. Let it be quiet, cool, and neutral.

I've paved my walkways with dark gray-maroon bricks, but flagstone could have been used. Flagstone is, however, difficult to fit into small geometric spaces, as I found when I tried to do so. My stones, being the flat slatey sort that occur on our property, are of different thicknesses as well as shapes. After several hours of hot work, trying not only to fit them in but to set them so as to make a level surface, I gave up and went to buy paving bricks. If your walkways are to be wider and/or less rigidly defined than mine, you might very well opt for flagstone. If your garden is large and you don't mind mowing, you could have grass paths. Keep in mind that they will have to be edged periodically as well as mowed. I have a motor-powered edging machine that cuts a fine line, but one still has to get down on hands and knees to lift out the roots and grass that have been cut off and trim the edge of what remains.

2

THE PLANTS—
MOSTLY ANNUALS
HERE

I realized early on when drawing up plans for the new garden that very few northern perennials come in blazing colors; they tend to be as restrained as the people. Those planning to create a hot-color extravaganza must use as many perennials as possible, then look to the tropics or semitropics for annuals, bulbs, tubers, and vines. This entails a certain amount of trouble for northern gardeners, who must dig and store bulbs and tubers over the winter—unless they would prefer to buy fresh ones every year. They'll have, as well, to raise annuals indoors and under lights each spring. Sometimes it's possible to find someone at a local greenhouse or garden center who will do this job for you. Since the choice of annuals to be found in six-packs at most garden centers is limited to petunias, marigolds (tagetes) of the puffy, spherical variety, blue lobelia, red salvia, and not much else, adventurous gardeners will have to find some way of producing those exotic creatures they'll encounter in Thompson and Morgan's—to say nothing of Park's, Stokes's, and Burpee's—seed catalogs. Of course there's just a chance that their garden center will offer trays of marigold 'Paprika' or 'Sunny Red' cosmos, or *Coleus* 'Molten Lava', described, almost alarmingly, by Thompson and

Facing north in the new garden. This was the summer when the marigold 'Naughty Marietta' tried to take over the garden.

Morgan as "the fiery hell of Molten Lava erupting and flowing in exquisite matte black and carmine-plum foliage." Might be nice in spite of the prose.

But assuming that your garden stores stick to the usual offerings, let's consider their red salvia—which will probably be the notorious *Salvia splendens.* This is the plant that is often found, as we said, marching along both sides of suburban front walks or trying (in vain) to beautify cement-surrounded planting areas in shopping malls. *Here* is where it belongs, in our new symphony, where hotter is better, where incendiary is appropriate. Breeders have concentrated so diligently on this species that early, midseason, and late, as well as short, midheight, and tallish, plants are to be had, many of them at garden centers, all of them endowed with excellent constitutions and a dogged determination to bloom ceaselessly, come what may, until cut down by a killing frost.

I put *Salvia s.* 'Laser Purple' in the new garden one year, and it wasn't a great success. But try it; you might do better with it than I did. 'Laser Purple' is not really purple but—all I can come up with is the color of the water you drain from shredded red cabbage. Not so flashy as *splendens,* but more elegant, is another salvia, S. *coccinea,* which bears small, scarlet, dragon's-mouth flowers on slender spikes measuring fifteen to eighteen inches. A more self-assertive version of this sage is S. *c.* 'Lady in Red'—really a terrific plant. I use it in sun and semishade, where it provides splashes of a pure red that "goes" either with the delicate border colors or the fiery ones of the new garden. It blooms from June right through the first frosts of autumn—through all of October, this year.

'Sunny Red' cosmos are almost essential for a hot garden, having delicate, glistening, one-and-a-half-inch-wide, single ray flowers in shades of orange and vermilion on one-and-a-half- to two-foot plants with dark, lacy leaves. Not at all like the large ordinary cosmos that come in white, rose, and mawkish mauve. These little cosmos are extremely pretty and often self-sow, saving you the trouble of tending a seed flat each spring, as long as you watch carefully for the seedlings in May.

Cosmos sulphureus 'Sunny Red' looks especially pretty against the purple foliage of a dahlia. The finely cut leaves of this cosmos are almost as attractive as its blossoms.

'Sunny Red' cosmos were developed from the species *Cosmos sulphureus*, familiarly known as Klondyke cosmos. Of these there is also 'Ladybird' mixed seed for flowers in red, orange, and yellow. Don't get 'Lemon Twist' (another Klondyke), but 'Sunny Gold' instead.

The only trouble I've had with this new project is that of having had to let go of some of my favorite prejudices. For years I've enjoyed scorning gladioli, dahlias, and marigolds—plants fit only for a public park (I thought). And as for geraniums (pelargoniums)—what real gardener would include them in his private paradise?

Further, I am on record as disapproving strenuously of breeders who double flowers until they look like shaggy puffballs regardless of their original design. Now here I am happily growing all the plants I sneered at and am even gazing fondly at the annual *Gaillardia pulchella* 'Red Plume' and feeling grateful to its breeder. Yet it looks not at all like a gaillardia, except for its leaves. From a low clump of these come, endlessly, six- to eight-inch stems bearing wonderful explosions of claret red. I've sold out—we all have our price.

'Red Plume' has a sibling called 'Yellow Plume'. If it performs as well as 'Red Plume', it will be most welcome. Another short, annual gaillardia is G. *pulchella* 'Yellow Sun'—whether single or double, we are not informed. There's a double mixture offered by one company, but mixtures are risky for a garden in which color is so important.

For some years there's been a mix-up between the British and the Americans, owing to an error in translation. The British call *Calendula officinalis* "marigold" or "pot marigold," and they call *Tagetes patula* and *T. erecta* "French marigolds" and "African marigolds," respectively (although they both originate in Mexico). Or they simply call them "tagetes." We call calendulas "calendulas" and both species of tagetes "marigolds." This has led to a certain amount of confusion, as when British lecturers in the United States show pictures of "marigolds" that are really, we say to ourselves, calendulas. Moreover, it has led American herb enthusiasts who have read British books to use tagetes blossoms as food, as food coloring, as flavoring, and as medicine, while they should be using *Calendula officinalis*, the plant that the British and other Europeans have traditionally used for these purposes.

Tagetes is revered in Mexico and India, where it adorns altars and has a role in religious ceremonies and festivals. It is sometimes used in cookery in India, Mexico, and parts of Africa.

Now that I've got that straightened out, I can proceed to discuss the two "marigolds" as garden plants. I grew up with calendulas, one of my mother's favorite plants. I have always loved them for their soft orange blossoms and their obliging habit of self-sowing. I've had them in the new garden from its beginning, when I raised a batch of them from a seed packet labeled 'Mandarin'. They've been fine, but this year I looked about to see what others I might try. One can still get seeds of the old species, C. *officinalis*, as well as various mixes of semidouble cream, yellows, and orange. The latter type wouldn't do here, but the species, being orange, would. Then there's a superstar named, for some reason, 'Radio Extra Selected', which was said to carry big, "cactus-dahlia-shaped" blooms of glowing orange on eighteen-inch stems. I decided to go for it but found it not as described. The plants are tall and bushy, but the blossoms are smaller, less full, and no more brilliant in color than those on my volunteer 'Mandarin' seedlings. Besides, the new plants take up too much room. I want to return to 'Mandarin' next year, but how will I know, now that I have added another strain, whose seedlings are whose? This time I should have left well enough alone. I should remind you here, perhaps, that one person's experience with a plant is not to be taken as the Word from on high. A plant that has performed badly for me may do very well for you, and vice versa. Much depends on weather, soil, situation, and skill, all of which vary. But to resume . . .

Calendulas do have one drawback: in hot, humid weather they tend to stop blooming. Deadheading them conscientiously every day will prolong the blooming period, of course, but you shouldn't rely on them after July if you live in a region of hot summers. Last summer the calendulas in my enclosed garden gave out in late summer, yet those in my daughter's garden, only a mile away, unenclosed on a windswept hill, went on beautifully until late autumn.

I can't resist adding that in Algeria I saw great *fields* of wild calendulas blazing

The centers of Dahlia 'Red Riding Hood' repeat the colors of the yarrow (Achillea 'Gold Plate'), the daylilies, and the calendula. The ubiquitous Salvia 'Victoria' calms it all down.

away under a sky of intense, ecstatic blue, all of them larger and more beautiful than any in my garden.

As for tagetes, I'm already using the little flat 'Disco' marigolds in red and orange. They're truly jewel-like, with their bright single blossoms sparkling against dark green, incised foliage—not at all like their round, rubbery relatives. Like the gaillardias, they seem never to stop blooming, even when they are not deadheaded, and will survive many frosts in the fall.

Gaillardia *'Red Plume' is in the foreground.* Lychnis *'Vesuvius'* and Dahlia *'Japanese Bishop' back up 'Disco Orange' marigolds.*

Single marigolds come in some pretty hectic combinations that I'm not sure I have the courage to take on. Have you seen 'Striped Marvel', with red-and-yellow petals striped, pinwheel fashion, from the center out? Well, I *said* I wanted wild colors, didn't I? Still, I hesitate. I may pusillanimously order twelve-inch 'Scarlet Sophie' instead. This isn't a ray flower, since it has rounded, slightly cupped petals. There are so many types of marigolds, one could fill the whole garden with them. Some of these small cultivars have semidouble, crested blooms. 'Safaris' look wonderful. Last summer I bordered the walkways with 'Naughty Marietta' instead of 'Disco' marigolds. 'Naughty Mariettas' are bright yellow with maroon-red blotches raying out from the center on each of their single lobed petals—just right, as to color and shape. But the bushes, which cover themselves continuously with these cheery blossoms, were really too big for their edging assignment. They grew up to two and a half feet and took up lots of the path as well as being too tall. But admittedly it was a strange summer; many things grew much taller than usual.

I was more pleased with 'Paprika', a charming miniature whose hundreds of blossoms measure not much more than half an inch across. They have wine-red, single petals edged with gold, while from a red center rises a tiny tuft of gold stamens. The plant forms a one-foot globe.

One more marigold I've been growing is 'Favourite', a single medium yellow whose two-inch blossoms also have a center tuft of dark gold stamens. The mounded plants measure about twenty by twenty inches. Nice.

When my garden was new, I looked for a small plant I could use to edge the walks and soften the rigid lines of the boards that define them and retain the soil of the planting areas. Before I discovered 'Disco' marigolds, I used *Sanvitalia procumbens*, known to some as creeping zinnia. This is an amiable little thing with opposite, dark green leaves on low, slowly spreading stems that carry countless small, dark-centered, yellow-orange daisies. Pleasant enough, but not calculated to

From this angle the hypericum, upper left, can hardly compete with the froth of marigolds, but Dahlia 'Border Princess' (center rear) is outshone by no other flower. This way and to the right of the princess is a mound of the charming miniature marigold 'Paprika'.

make the heart beat faster. I've been meaning to try California poppies (eschscholzia) as edging plants. How delicious they are, with their blue-green foliage and silky flowers! Poppies have an almost ingenuous, guileless, innocent appeal that no other flower has, somehow. The strain *Eschscholzia aurantiaca* 'Orange King' would be best, perhaps. There is no problem about their tolerating heat and full sun, but I do question their ability to keep the color coming all through summer and fall as the marigolds do. Here in the Northeast, in autumn, we often have periods of awfully cold, wet weather that might not be acceptable to natives of California. Besides, they do have a tendency to flop, which is not a desirable characteristic for an edging plant.

In Europe the wild red poppy of Flander's Field and elsewhere (*Papaver rhoeas*), sometimes known as corn poppy (the plant from which Shirley poppies were developed), grows, as I recall, about two feet tall and is of a red that inclines to scarlet rather than crimson. Their sole drawback is that they bloom for a few weeks only, in spring or summer. They are so beautiful while they last that one could certainly afford them a generous patch or two of garden space with the idea of slipping some already flowering annuals (which one would forehandedly have arranged to have waiting in pots) into the ground to replace them as they leave. Nothing could be simpler than growing annual poppies from seed; one has but to sprinkle the seed thinly over the prepared ground in late fall or early spring, then make sure to be brave enough to scuff up or pull out enough of the seedlings to allow the plants that remain to attain their full growth. If you must raise your seedlings indoors, sprinkle the seeds onto prepared peat pots, for poppies don't like to have their roots disturbed. When they are ready to set out, peel back a bit of the top of the pot and break open the bottom. Sometimes peat pots dry out after being planted and prevent the roots from spreading out.

Which reminds me of Celia Thaxter, who, in the last century, lived in Maine but gardened on the Isle of Shoals. She raised her seedlings at home, then carried them across to the island when the season for gardening came around. Since there were no peat pots in her day, she used eggshells for her poppies, which was clever of her.*

If the summers where you live are reasonably cool and dry, you can grow nemesia, a native of Africa that, exasperatingly enough, finds the heat and humidity that most of us in the United States have to endure not to its taste. I suppose it

---

*Celia Thaxter, *An Island Garden* (Boston: Houghton Mifflin, 1988).

sits on top of a mountain when it is at home, for, like those tricky alpines, it wants to grow in full sun. It's a lovely thing—you're lucky if you can grow it. It's suitable for either beds or containers. One listed as *N. nana compacta* 'Orange Prince', a form of *N. strumosa*, is a seven- to eight-inch plant with short racemes of one-and-a-half- to two-inch-wide flowers whose color has been described as "startling." There's seed, too, for one called 'Triumph Red'. These plants have slender, toothed, opposite leaves and two-lipped blossoms with cleft or notched petals.

We are going to talk about perennial coreopsis later, but have you ever grown those that are admittedly annuals? (I have trouble wintering over the perennials.) There's a twelve- to fourteen-inch, bright golden coreopsis (*C. basalis*, or *drummondii*) with a deep red center that looks good. It's called 'Golden Crown', and the blossoms are three inches wide. The same seed company that sells it has seed also for *C. tinctoria*, a dwarf, in mixed colors: "vibrant" yellow, red, and mahogany. They don't claim that it is perennial, so I assume it's going to be here for a summer only.

Tithonia rotundifolia 'Goldfinger' is one of the best annuals I've found for the new garden, although it can grow to a whopping five to six feet and is quite broad. Its large, ruffled, velvety, lance-shaped (not round) leaves set off beautifully the three- to four-inch ray flowers with their blunt, bright orange petals and crested, yellow centers. One does have to groom it pretty constantly, cutting off spent flowers and yellowing leaves. It may well be that if it were living under what it considered to be ideal conditions, it would never become untidy.

Gomphrena 'Strawberry Fayre' (or 'Strawberry Fields') was invented just in time for this color scheme, bearing, as it does, knobs of lively orange-red, instead of rose, dirty white, and magenta, which used to be the only colors in its repertoire. These never seem to fade but are as everlasting in life as in death.

The annual *Chrysanthemum* 'Zebra', in red and yellow, is welcome. So far, I've been able to find only one company that sells seed of annual chrysanthemums. I've been growing their *C. coronarium* 'Primrose Gem' in the long border, where its

*T*ithonia *blossoms, both fresh and spent, with* Gomphrena *'Strawberry Fayre'.*

clusters of delicious fresh, pale, really primrose-yellow blossoms have been a god-send during the dog days when many of the perennials look so depressed. Now I find there's a C. *c.* 'Golden Gem', just right for the new garden. These chrysanthemums bear their clusters of small daisy flowers on fourteen- to sixteen-inch stems. Give them good, rich soil and let them not lack for water during hot, dry days, and you will be richly rewarded. *C. dunnettii luteum* is also deep yellow and has larger double and semidouble flowers. (The "gems" have semidouble flowers with disk centers.) This plant has not been given a trade name but is offered under its botanical name only. It will attain a little more than two feet in height.

Rudbeckia 'Marmalade' is a great, gorgeous English annual that is much flashier than the old perennial standby *R.* 'Goldsturm' (a plant that could certainly also be used). 'Marmalade' stands only twenty-four inches high, making a well-formed, bushy plant that is constantly covered with four-inch orange daisies with conical, dark brown centers—the brightest and cheeriest black-eyed Susans you ever saw. The company that sells seed for this plant has seed for many other annual rudbeckias, tall and short, single and double. I like the sound of some called 'Rustic Dwarfs', twenty-one-inch plants with "rich" gold, bronze, yellow, and mahogany daisies with black cones. Might be a good alternative to gloriosa daisies if you are, like me, a little leery of them. Some of them seem just too big (seven inches across) and bold for all but the most daringly designed gardens. Yet, given the right amount of space and the right plants to surround them, gloriosa daisies might provide more drama than any of the other plants. I do think they would have to be carefully placed, and that would be *not* near the rich, elegantly clad dahlia 'Bishop of Llandaff', for example; their rough-hewn simplicity, their size, and their insistent stare would destroy the refined atmosphere around the bishop. In a large garden they could be grown against or with groups of double, deep yellow perennial helianthus and heliopsis, and with heleniums. It seems to me that when I had gloriosa daisies in the nursery some years ago, they weren't so large and overpowering as they are now. Isn't the situation getting a bit out of hand?

Eight- to ten-inch plants whose restrained growth habit makes them suitable for growing in containers as well as in the flower bed are *Rudbeckia hirta* 'Becky Mix'. The daisies are large and sprightly looking, each having a dark center disk. The only hazard is that the mix includes lemon yellow as well as darker shades tending toward orange. If one raised them oneself, rather than picking them from a blooming assortment at a garden store, one would have to plant the seeds early so that one could choose only the deeper colors for this special garden.

Another daisy, gazania (G. *ringens*), is smaller and subtler than gloriosa, having slender petals and sophisticated combinations of warm, jewel-like colors. I was quite distressed when, in the new garden, mine fainted away after having exhausted

*T*wo 'Sunny Red' cosmos with the splendid Rudbeckia 'Marmalade'.

A nice mixture of annuals: Rudbeckia hirta 'Irish Eyes' and Salvia coccinea.

themselves by having brought forth a flower or two on each plant. They certainly couldn't have objected to the heat—the plant is used as a ground cover in California, after all. I had thought perhaps gazania was another of those tropical plants that huddles in ravines or under the shade of banyan trees in its native land. Having asked myself what ailed it, I looked it up (which I should have done before planting it) in *Taylor's Guide to Annuals*. *Taylor's* says that it is a native of South Africa, and that it will perish after first blooming in hot, humid conditions unless provided with excellent drainage. Another time I'll try it in a container.

Seed for Transvaal daisies, or *Gerbera jamesonii* 'Super Giant Hybrids', can be found for plants of various colors, some of them ours. These are perennial in zone 8, with protection, and have a long blooming period. Their care, however, appears to be somewhat specialized—easy if you know how. The seeds take anywhere from eighteen weeks to three and a half months to make blooming plants. These must be set high in the ground, since they are susceptible to crown rot. They are deep-rooted, so dislike disturbance. They sound to me to be good for gardeners in the South or for those with greenhouses. The flowers are very beautiful, especially those that have not been drastically doubled by the breeders. If I lived on a hill in southern California, I'd plant lots of gerberas.

It's too bad that nasturtiums dislike being roasted. When I planted them in full sun in the new garden, I had to discard them in midsummer when their foliage turned yellow and their flowers wispy. The next year I put some next to the south wall of the garden, where they were in shade much of the time. They didn't do much all summer, but when the weather cooled off toward the end of August they crept out over the walkway and began to bloom. In climates where the summers get very hot, they really should be planted in pots so they can be moved. They can be placed in full sun in the early spring and moved into part shade during the middle of summer. Moved back into full sun when the weather grows cooler, they will revive, and carry blossoms until the first killing frost.

Another failure was *Helianthus* 'Velvet Queen', which grew gawkily to about six feet before putting out a flower or two, sort of as an afterthought. True, they were of a good russet red, but 'Velvet Queen's' real aim in life is to make a tall, stout, bristly stem, scantily clothed with leaves, which are saved for the top where they serve to obscure the flowers. The breeders of this one had better go back to the drawing board.

I'm not sure I've really had it with annual helianthus, as I'm toying with the idea of trying *H.* 'Orange Sun', a three-and-a-half-foot plant with very double flowers. If I do succumb and order seeds for it, I'll set the plants out in a holding bed so as to make sure they deserve garden space. A person with a small garden learns to be wary.

If you can contemplate growing a flower whose name is 'Teddy Bear' and which is said by one of its vendors to be "cuddly," you can get seed of a "very dwarf" (two-foot) helianthus that supports six-inch extra-double golden blossoms that are certainly—well, impressive.

Seed is offered to more conservative gardeners for a single, deep yellow helianthus, 'Sunspot', to be used as a bedding or container plant. This one is about sixteen to twenty-four inches tall. Actually, it may be better for a child's garden, as it makes ten-and-a-half-inch-wide, seed-bearing heads. Appears to be a regular sunflower with its legs cut short.

Last summer I saw at the Cornell herb garden two kinds of zinnias that sent me back to studying zinnia lists in seed catalogs. One of them was a large, fringed, imposing, blazing orange specimen called 'Torch' and the other a small double called 'Red Lollipop', both from Burpee. I can't find 'Torch' in this year's listing, but I note with satisfaction that one can order seeds for flowers in separate colors (from Park, Burpee, and Stokes).

I've found that there are many zinnias to choose from: there are giant "dahlia-flowered" series and tiny pom-pom types. There are zinnias striped in red and

Zinnia 'Torch' consorts with German chamomile in the herb garden at Cornell University.

yellow—goodness! You'll have to exercise control if you don't want to find yourself having to build an addition to the new garden—or going into the cut-flower business. One can grow old-fashioned Mexican zinnias, too, or *Zinnia linearis (angustifolia)*, a smooth, slender, eight-inch species that never stops bringing forth its one-and-a-half-inch orange blossoms. I grew these in a holding bed last summer and thought their color to be a bit too much on the tangerine side to work perfectly in my garden.

This last summer I failed to take my own advice and ordered too many zinnia seeds—eight kinds, actually—and had so many plants that I had to line out lots of them in a holding bed. That was really a good thing after all, because I was able to see how they behaved in both crowded and uncrowded conditions, the garden being jam-packed and the holding bed being roomier and airier. I also had extra plants to use where other individuals had either finished or fizzled (for example, beside campanulas or daylilies that had stopped blooming or in the spot where the chipmunks had eaten all my *pumilum* lilies).

If, like me, you've never grown zinnias before, and if, like me, you've always sped swiftly past their section in seed catalogs, you may be as ignorant as I was about their varieties and virtues. I grew the three-and-a-half-foot 'Big Red', whose flaming, fat flowers were nearly six inches across, and the fifteen-inch, slender-stemmed 'Old Mexico', with small, mahogany red, semidouble blossoms with frayed, gold-tipped petals. Twenty-inch 'Dashers' in scarlet and orange were of the large, imposing type, very double, while some of the 'Peter Pans' were less so, showing, as a consequence, yellow centers. Most unusual was Z. 'Pinwheel Orange', a single clear and clean daisy. I plan to grow it again next year, when I also mean to try one called 'Star Orange' that looks similar.

Zinnia 'Old Mexico' is a small flower that makes its presence felt.

I did have slug and tarnish beetle damage on some of the zinnias—oddly enough, more on the plants in the holding bed than on those in the crowded garden. The only explanation I can come up with is that during the exceptionally hot, dry summer, I gave more water to the garden than to the holding bed. I know that healthy plants appeal less to insects than ailing ones do (although *why* is a mystery), but still—wouldn't slugs prefer damper conditions? Luckily, the damage wasn't serious.

Red or rhubarb chard is used in flower as well as vegetable gardens, where space is not a problem.

How do you feel about putting red chard in your flower garden? It is done, you know, and by the very best gardeners. I've seen ruby chard looking at its ease and as if sure of striking just the right note in more than one purple-and-red border. It *is* the right color, at least during spring and early summer. If I don't use it in my own garden, it is because space is so limited I must reserve it for only the most glorious subjects, and also, perhaps, because I'd rather enjoy it as it grows in my husband's vegetable garden, where it keeps company with the blue-green blades of leeks, dark bouquets of broccoli, and ruffled heads of purple cabbage. Still, if you don't have a vegetable garden to put it in, you might perfectly legally grow it with your flowers. I would put leeks in my long border if I had room.

Ornamental peppers come in purple, red, and yellow. This one is called 'Treasure Red'.

Ornamental peppers are frequently grown in greenhouses for the Christmas trade, but you might find some for sale in summer. *Capsicum annuum* 'Treasure Red', 'Christmas Pepper', 'Fiesta', 'Vietnamese Hot Purple', and others can be grown from seed by people who are braver than I am after reading up on their culture. In the first place, they take four to six months to mature from seed (those grown for Christmas are planted in February). If you plant seed in April, with luck you'll have plants ready to perform in September. And these are *annuals*, remember. As seeds and seedlings, they must be kept at temperatures of around seventy degrees, night and day. When, in summer, you plant them outdoors, Stokes's catalog says you must "keep them well-sprayed against aphids." You are told they need a constant feeding program during fruit set. They are amusing and colorful plants, surely, but I think I'll leave their propagation to the professionals.

Those people with lots of space might want to add an especially tropical aspect to their gardens by planting the castor bean, *Ricinus communis*, whose gigantic (up to three feet across), palmately lobed leaves make any garden look like a painting by Gauguin or the Douanier Rousseau. In Africa, its home, this plant makes a forty-foot tree, but here it is grown as an annual. Seed for several varieties is offered, for plants with variously colored leaves and stems, growing from five to fifteen feet tall, plants that must be spaced from four to ten feet apart. *R.* 'Carmencita' is especially handsome, making a six-by-ten-foot shrub that has dark reddish brown leaves and two-foot panicles packed with round, red flowers shaped like sea urchins, followed by spiny seed pods.

You might want to use a native euphorbia in your garden, *Euphorbia heterophylla*, a spurge that is found throughout a large area from Illinois to Florida. It's a not-very-shapely but undeniably colorful three-foot plant, whose main attraction is its large upper leaves, which are blotched with red, giving it its common names of annual poinsettia and painted spurge (euphorbia). Like most annuals, it comes readily from seed.

Notwithstanding one's determination to rise manfully above prejudice of all kinds, one may not always succeed 100 percent. I won't say that when I read in a seed catalog "a useful bedding plant for extra dry areas—gas stations, traffic islands, etc.," I felt that I had received any encouragement in my efforts to accept amaranthus as a respectable genus. One has to give it credit for having some species that provide food, but is it enough to outweigh the curse of the weeds it burdens us with—pigweed and tumbleweed among them? Of course what I'm really thinking of are the two species, *tricolor* and *caudatus*, that have given us Joseph's coat with its leaves of red, yellow, and green and love-lies-bleeding (a most offensive name, don't you think?) with its very long, red, drooping, furry panicles. Both

What a gorgeous plant is 'Carmencita', a cultivar of the castor plant, Ricinus communis.

of these plants are . . . admired by many people. And those who wish to include them in their hot-color gardens are free to do so. They may also want to plant celosia, both the feathery, plumy kind and the kind that looks a little like velvet-textured brains or wrinkled upholstery. But since celosia is another genus that has never managed to inspire me with any feeling other than distaste, I disclaim all responsibility. Nevertheless, having now seen how beautifully amaranthus and celosia have been dealt with in the gardens of Wave Hill and Stonecrop, I feel that I may have been too hasty in condemning the genera. Obviously, in the hands of an artist, almost any plant can be used to good effect.

At Wave Hill this extravagant amaranth (Amaranthus hypochondriacus) *works wonderfully well with Russian sage and red dahlias.*

Celosia plumosa *is admired by many gardeners and is available in vibrant reds and yellows as well as in less strident colors.*

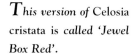

This version of Celosia cristata *is called 'Jewel Box Red'.*

I hope that I have not, by these outspoken comments, raised up a host of enemies against me. But how could I have helped it? Should I have said I thought amaranthus and celosia beautiful even though I don't? Or said nothing? When I remember how cross I get with Wyman* when he calls a plant I like "not garden-worthy," and that I'm still holding it against Christopher Lloyd that in one of his books he made some disparaging remarks about heather, I fear the consequences of my candor. Could it be that other people feel as strongly about amaranthus and celosia as I do about heather? Gardeners become so defensive about their dear plants, as if they were part of the family. However, I find myself now in the same position as Mr. Lloyd, who, after speaking negatively about heather, went on to say: "Their adoring public will heartily disagree and are welcome to do so, but it's no good looking to me for kind words that would stick in my gullet." ("Heather," he adds, "is for grouse.")†

* Donald Wyman, *Wyman's Gardening Encyclopedia* (New York: Macmillan, 1980).

† *Foliage Plants* (London: Collins, 1973), pp. 68–69.

PLANT LIST: ANNUALS

1   *Amaranthus caudatus, A. tricolor*

2   *Beta vulgaris* var. (ruby chard)

3   *Calendula officinalis* and others

4   *Capsicum annuum* 'Treasure Red', 'Christmas Pepper', 'Fiesta', 'Vietnamese Hot Purple'

5   *Celosia cristata, C. plumosa*

6   *Chrysanthemum* 'Zebra', *C. coronarium* 'Golden Gem', *C. dunnettii luteum*

7   *Coreopsis basilis (drummondii)* 'Golden Crown', *C. tinctoria*

8   *Cosmos sulphureus* 'Sunny Red', 'Sunny Gold'

9   *Eschscholzia aurantiaca* (California poppy) 'Orange King'

10 *Euphorbia heterophylla* (painted spurge, annual poinsettia)

11 *Gaillardia pulchella* 'Red Plume'

12 *Gerbera jamesonii* 'Super Giant Hybrids'

13 *Gomphrena* 'Strawberry Fayre' (sometimes called 'Strawberry Fields')

14 *Helianthus* 'Orange Sun', *H.* 'Teddy Bear'

15 *Nemesia nana compacta* 'Orange Prince' (*N. strumosa*), *N.* 'Triumph Red'

16 *Papaver rhoeas* (Flander's Field or corn poppy)

17 *Ricinus communis* 'Carmencita' (castor bean)

18 *Rudbeckia* 'Marmalade', 'Rustic Dwarfs', 'Becky Mix'

19 *Salvia splendens, S. coccinea, S. c.* 'Lady in Red'

20 *Tagetes* (marigold) 'Disco Red', 'Disco Orange', 'Naughty Marietta', 'Paprika', 'Favourite', 'Scarlet Sophie'

21 *Tithonia rotundifolia* 'Goldfinger'

22 *Tropaeolum* (nasturtium) 'Empress of India' and others

23 *Zinnia* 'Peter Pan' and 'Dasher' series, 'Torch', 'Big Red', 'Old Mexico', 'Pinwheel' series, *Z. linearis (angustifolia)*

3

THE PLANTS: PERENNIALS

As I've said, there are simply not a lot of flaming northern perennials, but we'll do our best with what we have. There *are* plenty of yellows, certainly—lots of sunflowery things, to begin with. These are not like the heavy-headed giant that is grown for human consumption, oil, and birdseed, but garden cultivars of helianthus and heliopsis that are much more refined.

Beginning and sometimes even veteran gardeners are apt to feel a certain amount of exasperation as they struggle to master plant names, due to the fact that so many of them begin with "heli" (helianthus, helianthemum, heliopsis, heliotrope, helichrysum—to name a few). Understanding that most of the helis get their names from *helios*, the Greek word for sun, is some, but not very much, comfort. It at least indicates to the gardener that the plant might want full sun. You

wouldn't plant something that begins with "heli" in the woods garden or on the north side of the house without looking it up.

So, let's begin with a couple of helis: heliopsis and helianthus. The American native, heliopsis, *H. helianthoides,* or false sunflower, is nice out by the barn but too weedy for the garden. However, cultivars that have been derived from it are excellent, long-blooming, exuberant, and most desirable individuals. I've a fine double one, 'Summer Sun', which is listed sometimes under *H. helianthoides* or its subspecies *scabra.* It seems to be a kind of strain rather than a cultivar, as it comes in and is offered as single, semidouble, or double. I ordered two plants and got one semidouble and one double. They are both fine specimens, growing to around four feet and carrying fluffy, three-inch golden blossoms for weeks and weeks, starting in July, without ever looking tired or shabby. 'Summer Sun' is a real winner.

A plant I got as *Heliopsis helianthoides* 'Golden Plume' was shorter (three feet), had larger double blossoms, but didn't stay with me for more than two or three years. No reason for its resignation was given, so, as usual, I'm afraid I did the wrong thing though I was consoled somewhat when I read in Armitage (*Herbaceous Perennial Plants*)* that heliopsis is a short-lived perennial. I had *H. h.* 'Golden Greenheart' for a while, too. Both of these are splendid plants. You should try them, or some of the other good heliopsis cultivars. A new German called 'Ballerina' ('Spitzentanz-erin') sounds good. It's a sturdy, compact plant with shiny, dark green leaves. The double flowers begin to appear early in June and continue through September.

There are many species of the mostly American genus helianthus, some of them hardy only in the South. Clausen/Ekstrom say of helianthus, "These robust

* Allan M. Armitage, *Herbaceous Perennial Plants* (Athens, Ga.: Varsity Press, 1989).

One Helianthus *'Velvet Queen' peers out over a mass of the long-blooming* Heliopsis *'Summer Sun'. In the foreground are perilla and the dark-foliaged* Dahlia *'Ellen Houston'.*

This oxeye daisy is **Heliopsis helianthoides *'Karat'*.**

---

plants are suitable for the back of the border or for naturalizing in less formal areas. They are rather coarse and garish and should be used with discretion if they are not to overpower their neighbors."* Exactly. Which is why they go so well in a hot-color garden, where we will not make use of any of the species, which bear single sunflowers and are often invasive, but will choose from the many fine garden cultivars, most of which are well-behaved doubles and semidoubles. *H. atrorubens* 'The Monarch' is a semidouble whose yellow ray flowers have dark purple centers. This five- to six-foot plant with long, toothed, hairy leaves is for southerners, being hardy only as far north as zone 8. Most of the other popular cultivars have been derived from *H. x multiflorus* (*H. annuus x H. decapetalus*). My *H. x. m.* 'Flore Pleno'

* Ruth R. Clausen and Nicolas H. Ekstrom, *Perennials for American Gardens* (New York: Random House, 1989), p. 269.

produces great golden blossoms that are almost the size and shape of "football mums." It requires plenty of room as, when located in rich soil and given its head, it can grow six feet tall by four feet wide. Five-foot 'Loddon Gold' is for zones 4–9 and will give you round, double "anemone-centered" flowers in September, while eight-foot hardy *H. maximiliani* will carry three-inch, single sunflowers from August until frost. Doesn't sound very flashy, that last one. Might be nice out by the pasture fence, but I'd go for 'Loddon Gold' for the garden. Avoid 'Capenock Star', which is lemon yellow.

Two big yarrows provide sheets of yellow for many weeks—*Achillea filipendulina* 'Gold Plate' and A. 'Coronation Gold', both of which I always found too strong in color for the border but now value highly. They're good, stout individuals that always look tidy, besides being generous with their blooms and needing almost nothing in the way of food and drink.

It might be wise to warn you here about the new German yarrows that are sold as named plants (A. 'Paprika', 'Heidi', 'Hope', etc.) or as seed for a strain called 'Débutante'. (Actually I am only guessing that the seed results from the work of German breeders.) In many ways these are very good plants; the flowers are exceptionally large and look almost like clusters of daisies—and they come in marvelous new colors. I've tried quite a few of them and even put 'Paprika' in the new garden, then took it out again. The trouble with them is that the flowers fade to quite different colors that are not what one wanted in the color scheme. If one lived in Germany, where the summers are benign rather than brutal, these lovely yarrows might not change color so drastically. Or if one had a gardener who would take care to remove the altered flower heads immediately. Now you may have grown German yarrows and found them perfect. Perhaps in Oregon? Or even Illinois? I can only tell it as it has been for me.

Catalogs offer several yellow heleniums, and more appear every year as the busy Germans work away on them. I've had solid yellow 'Butterpat' for years and can find

*P*art of horticulturist Nancy Goodwin's garden is a celebration of yellows, sparked here and there with red and orange. The smooth-leaved species Zinnia angustifolia *is in front,* Helianthus angustifolius *in back,* Cosmos sulphureus *here and there.*

no fault with it, but it might be fun to try 'Kugelsonne' or 'Zimbelsterne', both yellow, the first with chartreuse disks, the second with touches of bronze. 'Waldtraut' is described in one list as having orange flowers, and in another as having frilly, gold petals with touches of bronze surrounding a dark central cone. And there are more. All heleniums bloom in late summer or fall, with the chrysanthemums. They make excellent cut flowers, as well as garden plants, since their many one- to one-and-a-half-inch ray flowers are held in dense clusters or corymbs, on sturdy stems so that one cut stem furnishes a bouquet.

Red heleniums tend to be on the bronze side, which is fine, especially as some of them have yellow center disks or yellow or orange flecks on their petals. All the same, I want to try two new ones—'Crimson Beauty' and 'Dunkel Pracht'—which sound as if they might be of a redder red.

Heleniums, if grown in the moist soil they like and in full sun, will attain five feet or so and, depending on their location, may need staking. If you'd prefer a shorter, more compact plant, you can cut them to half their height in early July. This will delay their bloom, but not by much.

My experiences with the genus coreopsis have been fraught with frustration.

This summer everything grew enormously tall, for some reason. The yarrow is 'Gold Plate'. Lower left Gaillardia 'Red Plume'. The big clematis is C. x jackmanii, which does not here look as dark as it usually does.

I've grown the thread-leaf kind (*C. verticillata*) as well as many cultivars derived from other species, but the only ones that ever stood by me through good times and bad, year in year out, were that cheery little *C. auriculata* 'Nana' and *C. verticillata* 'Golden Showers'. True, the latter was inclined to be a little more enterprising than is desirable, but since its color was too warm for my cool border, it lived in a holding bed where it caused no serious trouble. Aside from these two, all other coreopsis have had their year or two of splendor, then have left the scene. If only plants could leave a suicide note so that we could find out what we did wrong! (Doesn't it seem, sometimes, as if all one's plants were hell-bent on either suicide or murder?) Or was it just that the cold, cruel world—at minus twenty degrees Fahrenheit—was too much for them? Or the heat?

As I wended my way through reference books, looking for light and answers to my coreopsis problems, I found, not much to my surprise, a muddle. To begin with, except for the thread-leaf cultivars such as 'Moonbeam' and 'Zagreb', named garden varieties are mostly derived from two species: *C. lanceolata*, which is found principally in the northern part of the United States; and *C. grandiflora*, a native of Georgia, Texas, Florida, and other southern states. These places of origin should make a difference as to the hardiness of the cultivar, yet many books and catalogs will say that *C.* 'Sunray' is a form of *C. grandiflora*, while others say it's a form of *C. lanceolata*. How to tell how hardy it may be? All catalogs I've seen call *C.* 'Early Sunrise' a perennial except for Thompson and Morgan, which says it's a perennial *or* half-hardy annual. A perennial in Virginia and a half-hardy annual in upstate New York? Then, to top it all, in *Hardy Herbaceous Perennials* by Leo Jelitto and Wilhelm Schacht, I read that 'Sunray', which they say is derived from the southern species, *C. grandiflora*, will perish *where summers are hot*. If one weren't so dogged, one would throw in the towel.

The thing to do about coreopsis, if you live in zone 5 or farther north and have had experiences similar to mine, is to grow the species *C. lanceolata*, *C. verticillata*

'Golden Showers', and C. *auriculata* 'Nana' as perennials and treat the German cultivars and the ones called 'Sunray' and 'Early Sunrise' like annuals or biennials. I've lost 'Early Sunrise' and 'Zagreb' in the new garden but am trying several 'Goldfinks' this year. If they are there next year, I'll be surprised.

But enough of yellow flowers, for the moment, except to add that there are heaps of good, strong, yellow and orange daylilies—in fact you can scarcely make a hot garden without them. I have many whose names have, sadly, been lost: a huge, orange-yellow one whose slender petals curve back like strips of peeling from a papaya, an old double orange streaked with red and other yellows. Of course I have also included the small, long-blooming 'Stella d'Oro'. But you can round up

I wish I knew the name of this glorious red daylily. Hypericum frondosum, *not daunted by the splendor of its neighbor, is bravely blooming, lower right.*

daylilies with appropriate coloring from your own garden, or order orange 'Chicago Sunrise' (six-inch flowers, one-and-a-half-foot plants), double gold 'Candilla' (four-and-a-half-inch flowers on twenty-inch plants), or 'Golden Prize' or 'Golden Gift' or 'Golden Chimes'. Just select a few with the most enticing descriptions, unless you live near a nursery and can see for yourself.

Daylilies also come in glorious reds these days—true, pure, strong reds, some of them with orange throats. It's really no use naming them, there are so many, but I can't resist mentioning 'Carey Quinn' and 'Red Rim'. I made the acquaintance of two dark red—almost black—ones at Stonecrop one summer: 'Latin Lover' and 'Ed Murray'. You can forgive them their names when you see their glowing, velvety petals.

Daylilies are not without their faults, you know, no matter what the nursery people say. You'll sometimes have to cut off ugly yellow leaves to make them tidy and remove the spent blossoms for the same reason. On the old-fashioned kinds, the flowers shrivel into slender twists that are not really unsightly, but the large, sumptuous new ones make a mushy mass that must be got rid of. If you put a flat stepping stone or two by your large daylilies, you can make them neat without compacting the soil around them too much.

Another drawback to the new cultivars, especially the large red and purple ones, is that the rain or the sprinkler spots them, making them extremely unsightly. If it's just a case of the gardener and her garden, the result is not serious, but if it's a garden to which visits by a photographer or a garden club have been scheduled, it makes for a certain amount of anxiety.

A perennial from Russia, *Lychnis chalcedonica*, carries some of the brightest scarlet flowers to be found anywhere. Its common name, Maltese cross, was given it on account of the shape of the deeply cleft petals. The flowers are carried in dense terminal clusters on straight, upright, twenty-inch stems (these, however, often topple over if not staked). I used to grow Maltese cross in the nursery but finally let it go, having become irritated with it for allowing its rather coarse leaves to turn brown as soon as the weather got hot and dry. But now I'm wondering if I shouldn't take it back into the fold; I could perhaps tuck it behind some bushy plants that would hide its shabby late-summer foliage. Actually, since I make sure that the new garden is never dry, the lychnis might go on looking respectable all season. Maltese cross is easily grown from seed, but plants are to be had from mail-order nurseries if you're in a hurry.

Lychnis x arkwrightii 'Vesuvius' is a hybrid that is listed as a perennial, but it often behaves like an annual in my garden. Luckily it self-sows, for its vivid orange-red flowers, which appear in late May and continue through June and part of July, give the first indication of the conflagration to come. I only wish the plants would bloom all summer. They provide not only fine flowers but good bronze-maroon foliage as well. I grew one last year, *L. migueliana,* that is similar to *arkwrightii* but shorter (ten inches rather than sixteen). It has somewhat redder flowers, if possible, and darker, wine-colored leaves. The foliage on both of these lychnis tends, however, to become green and tacky-looking as the summer progresses.

When monardas come into bloom they bring the hummingbirds careening into the new garden, where masses of 'Cambridge Scarlet' and 'Gardenview Scarlet' bee balms stand against giant, brilliant orange lilies. Add several gleaming, iridescent green and red hummingbirds to the floral composition, and you'll stand marveling at what God, and you, have wrought.

Some people fault monardas for their pushy ways, but I find it easy to forgive a feverish colonizer that is forthright, at least, in its methods. The stolons of these plants remain just under the surface of the ground and are easy to pull up. It's plants like *Artemisia ludoviciana* that I can't abide—plants that send stolons and roots way down under before popping them up in the middle of both near and far neighbors. So, except for the tendency of some of the monardas to mildew, I find them to be

The best time of year for the hummingbirds is the period when the bee balms are blooming. 'Cambridge Scarlet' is on the left, 'Gardenview Scarlet' on the right, Dahlia *'Border Princess' in the foreground.*

near perfect perennials. I like the explosive aspect of their blossoms; I'm sure they don't intend it but they look enthusiastic, somehow. And the colors of some of the newer ones are wonderful. 'Gardenview Scarlet' is really a rich crimson, and the color of its bracts and buds before the flowers open is almost as beautiful, being the color you would get if you mixed, on a palette, alizarin crimson with ivory black. I use M. 'Mahogany' in the garden, for its brownish red ties in with the purple-foliaged plants such as perilla. 'Adam' is a deep rosy pink that might work in some hot gardens, though not in mine.

Monarda 'Blue Stocking' (Blaustrumph) is a lovely thing in lavender. I thought

Monarda 'Blue Stocking' *is an excellent plant but is not a dark enough purple for this garden. 'Prairie Night' or 'Violet Queen' will replace it. There is one tithonia blossom against the fence.*

it would be dark enough for the new garden, but it is not. I'm going to work up the courage to fork it all out and replace it with M. 'Prairie Night', whose deep violet blossoms are better suited to the requirements of the color scheme.

Some euphorbias have a problem with intense heat and will do better in warm regions when protected from afternoon sun. One should also make sure they don't dry out. When I grew *Euphorbia griffithii* 'Fireglow', it made a somewhat sprawling, two-by-two-foot shrub whose long, slender leaves were distinguished by red midribs. In midsummer it topped each stem with clusters of flaming red-orange bracts. It was pretty nice, though certainly not as attractive as it is said to be by others who have grown it—but of course plants differ according to their environments and the treatment they receive. If you've seen it and admire it, try it now. It would be one more red-flowering perennial.

In my nursery I used to have a row of fire-engine red, two-foot penstemons I got as *Penstemon barbatus* 'Torre' from the wholesale nursery Sunny Border. According to Andersen's *Source List of Plants and Seeds*, a penstemon called 'Torreyi' is offered by Rocknoll Nursery.* It may be the same one. It's certainly worth looking for, because not only is it splendid in appearance but in performance as well. A couple of years ago I ordered a cultivar, *P. b.* 'Prairie Fire', which not surprisingly was said to have bright or at least salmon-red flowers, but having put three of them in the garden, I had to take them out again when they proudly produced apricot-pink bells. It could be that I was sent the wrong plants and should try again—with a different nursery.

Once I grew a lot of belamcandas from seed, both *B. chinensis*, the orange one with freckles, and *B. flabellata*, the yellow one without freckles. They were lovely—I was proud—until they contracted some mysterious ailment, became very sad and bedraggled, and failed to reappear the following spring. Was it botrytis, I wonder? Or borers? As you can see, I'm not a belamcanda expert, but you might succeed better with this tuberous subject than I, and they (especially *B. chinensis*) certainly would be a possibility for your new garden. These Oriental plants resemble and, in fact, are related to iris. They stand quite stiffly upright and, in early or midsummer, send up stems that bear upfacing clusters of orange flowers. The petals of *B. chinensis* are spotted and splashed with yellow and crimson. If space is at a premium in your garden, you might want to save it for longer-blooming subjects, since these small leopard lilies soon turn into blackberry lilies when they form pods that open to show shiny black seeds (much appreciated by makers of dried flower arrangements).

* Andersen Horticultural Library (Chanhassen: University of Minnesota Libraries, 1990–92).

*B*efore they make the fruit that gives them their alternate name of blackberry lilies, belamcandas display the markings that earned them the name leopard lilies.

Bearded iris (*I. germanica*) will furnish you, while they last, with rich gold as well as red and purple. You might prefer plants that bloom over a longer period, but if you have lots of room, if you adore iris, and if you have sweet, sandy soil so that the plants will not be as likely to suffer from borers and root rot, you could indulge yourself and order 'Inferno', a ruby red with an orange beard, 'Interpol', a purple-black, and 'Gold Galore'.

Siberian iris (*I. sibirica*) are easier to raise than the bearded. Instead of sweet, sandy soil, they prefer a dampish loam on the acid side, if anything. The more nourishment and water they get, the better they grow, but they'll grow, though less gloriously, even when neglected—the old-timers, that is. The fancier new ones don't, in my experience, show the stamina of their forebears. However, you can easily fit into your garden some clumps of the old purple 'Caesar's Brother'; they won't take up much room, and, since Siberians bloom later than bearded iris, they'll be better able to accompany your annuals. There are at least two newer dark purples, 'Ruffled Velvet' and 'Tealwood', that you might want to use. Unfortunately these iris don't, so far as I know, come in appropriate reds and yellows, the reds being too rosy and the yellows too pale.

But wait—there is a yellow Chinese iris, *I. forrestii,* that you can grow from seed if you're not in a hurry; iris sometimes take many months to germinate. This one looks as if it would be worth a wait. It has shiny, narrow leaves about fifteen inches high and produces, when it's ready, deep gold, purple-veined flowers.

Like Siberians, Japanese iris (*I. ensata*) furnish none of the reds and yellows we need. Rich purples are easy to find—'Dark Drapery' for one—but proper reds and yellows, no. There's a hybrid between *I. ensata* and *I. pseudacorus* named 'Rising Sun' whose yellow might be strong enough. If you keep lime away from Japanese iris, give them rich soil and full sun, and don't let them dry out, you'll find them splendid garden plants. I've raised lots of them from seed and have, as a result, flowers of many different colors and patterns; I must say that although they are not as huge and luscious as the named varieties I've bought, they are much better able to endure adversity. No doubt they are closer to their wild ancestors.

I'm not sure I did the right thing when I put some 'Fanal' astilbes into the new garden. I rather think they should come out—not because they're the wrong color but because the garden doesn't really get under way until well into July, when red astilbes are winding up their annual performance. Besides, a horticulturally canny friend told me they didn't look as if they belonged, and I think he was right. His reason was that they have a delicate north-woodland look that's out of place in a jungle. *Heuchera* 'Pluie de Feu' may be inappropriate for the same reasons and should probably also come out. I did have sense enough not to plant red tulips in this garden, knowing that they'd look pretty silly all by themselves when other garden inmates were either just emerging from the ground or hadn't even been planted yet.

In discussing perennials, I hardly know whether or not to include gaillardias, since with me they rarely behave as such. It may be that my soil is too heavy. Are they hardy for other people in zone 5? Whatever it is, I am obliged to keep buying them or raising them every year or so from seed. If they live through the second winter, I'm astonished and delighted. *Gaillardia x grandiflora* 'Burgundy' is a largish (two- to three-foot) floppy plant whose lax habit is redeemed by its soft, furry, burgundy-colored flowers. One does have to keep deadheading the plants and prop them up as well, but they deserve a little extra care. Most gaillardias are bicolors, one color banded on another: red and yellow, red and orange—just what we're looking for. I'm going to grow 'Goblin' again next year. It's a red-and-gold dwarf, as are 'Baby Cole' and 'Kobold'. I think the all-yellow 'Golden Goblin' is a bit too pale.

Cardinal flowers are growing in the woods garden near the entrance to the new garden, but I don't dare put them inside; they would surely hate the heat and lack of shade.

I'm not forgetting Oriental poppies (*Papaver orientale*), which do come in pure cadmium red now, as well as the flaming orange of the old species, either one of which would be grand in a large garden. They do take up a lot of space, especially when one takes into consideration their brief period of bloom. I've always thought that the place for those old-fashioned Oriental poppies is not in the border but massed against a woodland where their color can be given full value by having a dark background. There they could have their week or two of glory, then go slowly dormant, not bothering anybody or taking up valuable garden space. But if you have the room, why not include them?

You can buy plants or seeds for the dwarf 'Allegro', whose color is that of the species—hot orange—but which grows to only sixteen inches or so and is more inclined than most of its clan to stand erect.

The true red Oriental poppies go by such names as 'Bonfire' and 'Beauty of Livermore'.

A three- to four-foot poppy that holds itself up is *Papaver bracteatum*, a close relative (and believed by some to be a variety) of *P. orientale*. This is the most splendid poppy I know, its bloodred cups being as much as eight inches across. All around the Mediterranean, and especially in Turkey, they make great sweeps of glowing color, as far as the eye can see, in fields and olive groves—a sight that makes you catch your breath. I wonder if they would naturalize here, if they'd be able to cope with our tough immigrant weeds: burdock, teasel, wild carrot, and the rest? They should at least grow happily in our gardens. Thompson and Morgan has the seed.

We still haven't discussed perennial chrysanthemums (whose new names I refuse to accept). Surely we can find many with the right colors, even though they might not—in spite of being labeled "hardy mums"—be reliably hardy in the North. I rely on an old one called 'Aztec' that I got from Wayside Gardens, years ago when Wayside was under different management. I don't know anyone who sells it now, and it's a great pity, for it's one of the two or three chrysanthemums out of many I've tried that can be counted on to hang in there through our rough winters. It's a double, bright red and yellow, and it starts blooming early, usually in August, carrying on stalwartly until heavy frost. But of course there are hundreds of chrysanthemum cultivars, some of which may be hardy for you.

There are many species of chrysanthemums, but the showy ones we're looking for are hybrids and will be listed under *Chrysanthemum x morifolium* or *dendranthema*. These can range from twelve-inch cushions to plants two and a half feet tall in almost every color but pure blue. You'll find deep golden yellows, even orange ('Artisan', 'Happy Face', 'Flaming Sun') and fine dark reds ('Drummer Boy',

'Vampire', 'Fireside'). 'Vampire' is a Canadian introduction, thus may be expected to stand more cold than most of the others. You can help your chrysanthemums to survive cold winters by dividing the clumps every spring. It renews their strength if you lift the whole tangled mass and wiggle it apart soon after it has sent up new green leaves. You needn't worry about delaying its blooming time, for each morsel of leafy stem with good roots will make a full-sized blooming plant by fall. Above all, do not, if you live as far north as zone 5, buy blooming plants at the garden center in the autumn and expect them to be alive the following spring, unless you can overwinter them in a cold frame or greenhouse.

Butterfly weed (*Asclepias tuberosa*)—or butterfly flower, as it is now called—is one of the very few really orange hardy native perennials and certainly would be a candidate for a hot-color garden that has well-drained, rather spare soil. I put some in my garden, where they were unfortunately overwhelmed by exuberant daylilies and a giant tithonia when I forgot to protect them. Butterfly weed hates to have its roots disturbed; one has to start out, if not with seed planted in the ground, with plants from pots that are necessarily going to be on the small side. Put next to a bur-geoning tithonia that is spreading its skirts as it shoots swiftly skyward, a moderately sized, moderately paced asclepias doesn't have a chance. I'm thinking of building cages to make a sort of buffer zone around the ones I put in next year. It really is a jungle in there.

When I tried to germinate the seed of *Asclepias t.* 'Gay Butterflies'—a glorified and multicolored version of butterfly weed—I failed miserably. I'd have had at least partial success if I'd frozen or chilled the seed flat for several weeks, or if I'd had fresh seed. When I gathered seeds of plain *A. tuberosa* and planted them immediately, they came up like popcorn. Many nurseries list 'Gay Butterflies', but since their colors range through yellow, orange, scarlet, and pink, you'll have to make sure you get the colors you want. Some vendors may have them in pots, already blooming.

A South American asclepias, *A. curassavica,* has gone wild in some of our

Butterfly weed is one of the gayest and gaudiest of our native plants, a tough but classy milkweed.

southern states. It's three feet tall, has long, slender, shiny leaves, and carries loose umbels of flowers with red corollas and orange coronas. Its common name is blood-flower, and wouldn't it be welcome in a southern hot-color garden? So long as the pods were removed before the seeds took flight, perhaps.

I'm toying with the idea of trying a red-hot poker or two, although I'm not at all sure they'd like it here. Gardeners farther south could confidently install vermilion and yellow *Kniphofia* 'Royal Standard' or orange-and-yellow *K.* 'Shenandoah'. One Maryland nursery says the latter is very hardy—but "very hardy" might not mean to them what it does to me. Kniphofia is another plant I've been jeering at for years; I'd feel that 'Shenandoah' was behaving very charitably if it consented to grow for me.

Hibiscus grew, with oleander and agapanthus, amongst the broken marble Roman columns and sarcophagi in the garden of a house we once lived in on the Punic Ports in Carthage, but never (except for the wild *Hibiscus moscheutos palustris*) in my North American garden, where I thought it would look too exotic. Yet now that I'm into exotic, I'm giving hibiscus another look. There are many large-flowered hybrids derived from three species, *H. moscheutos*, *H. coccineus*, and *H. militaris* (often listed as cultivars of *moscheutos*), which claim to be hardy through zone 5. The best of these, for our purposes at least, is 'Lord Baltimore'. If you think your garden can handle a four- to five-foot perennial with ten-inch-wide, hollyhock-shaped, fiery red flowers, why not go for it? It will need plenty of space and moisture, too, but when it's satisfied it should bloom nonstop from July through fall, since it is sterile and won't be spending its time making seed. Available as plants or seed is a more restrained series called 'Disco Belle' whose nine-and-a-half-inch flowers, described in the catalog as "parasol-like," are held above two-and-a-half-foot plants. Still sounds pretty startling. These can be found in separate colors, including red, or as a mix. The four-foot 'Southern Belle' strain with ten-and-a-half-inch flowers seems to be available only as seed and only in mixed colors. *H. coccineus*, a native of our Southeast, bears six- to eight-inch flowers of deep red and has most attractive lobed, palmate leaves. It's more tender than the others we've mentioned.

While we are speaking of Malvaceae—what about hollyhocks? It's true they're not reliably perennial and they do suffer from flea beetles and rust, so if you object to using chemical sprays and have not yet found alternate solutions you might not want to consider *Alcea* (or *Althaea*) *rosea* 'Chater's Scarlet'. If you could solve its problems, this stately specimen with double, fiery red flowers would assuredly add panache to your garden, especially if it's accompanied by a group of the stunning black hollyhocks *A. r.* 'Nigra'. Maybe the rusty perforated leaves wouldn't show if you had enough bushy plants in front of them.

If you delight in grasses and like to combine them with perennials and annuals, you'll probably want to include a few of the red ones in your hot-color composition. Remember, though, that they don't look really blood red unless the sun is shining through (not on) them, and even then they don't look anywhere near as red as catalog pictures make them appear. If you can put them in a high spot that catches the evening sun, you will show them to their greatest advantage. I put my Japanese blood grass, *Imperata cylindrica* 'Red Baron', of which I am very fond, in the new garden, but have decided to move it somewhere else next spring. It would certainly be welcome if the garden were larger, but I've simply got to use every square foot for plants with more éclat than my little 'Red Baron' can muster. You might prefer a taller (four- to five-foot) red switchgrass, *Panicum virgatum* 'Rotstrahl-Busch' or

P. v. 'Haense Herms'. The trouble with them is that they'll not turn red until late in the season—probably September. One that is less hardy (zones 6–9) as well as being a different shade of red is *Miscanthus sinensis* var. *purpurascens*. This three- to four-foot grass also gains color through the summer, becoming deep purple-red by autumn.

A very good ornamental grass, purple fountain grass (*Pennisetum setaceum* 'Atrosanguineum'), seems to be listed now only by wholesale

*J*apanese blood grass should be sited, if possible, where the sun will shine through it.

In this private garden Sedum 'Rosy Glow', Japanese blood grass, and Ajuga 'Bronze Beauty', reiterating red, rose, and burgundy, hold the composition together.

nurseries. Northern gardeners needn't try to get hold of it, for it likes warmer winters than they can give it. Of course it could be treated as an annual in cold climates.

While we're dealing with grasses (even though this one belongs in the next chapter), what about black mondo grass? Well, it's really a kind of lily, but since it looks like a grass and acts like a grass, I'm going to treat it as a grass. Its impressive name is *Ophiopogon planiscapus* 'Nigrescens' (*O. p. arabicus*), and it is also a bit tender, being listed for zones 6–9. It's said to be six to eight inches tall, so I wonder what mine is. A friend brought me one (without a marker) that never grows taller than four or five inches. It's hardy, too—doesn't complain of the cold, though that

Fluffy flowers of purple fountain grass (Pennisetum setaceum 'Atrosanguineum') *drape themselves gracefully over a yellow zinnia.*

may be the reason it is short and not much interested in making flowers. The fact that it's growing near a locust tree might also have something to do with it. (Locust trees are greedy for food and water.) Black mondo grass often hides small, lilac flowers and later its black berries among its leaves.

I have the uneasy feeling that I'm sticking biennials in with both perennials and annuals. But then, biennials are bothersome to classify. Some bloom the first year, most not until the second. Some die right after flowering, some in their second winter—and some go on briskly for several years, pretending to be perennials. Of course a lot depends upon soil, drainage, climate, and the kind of weather you happen to be having.

But let's talk about all kinds of dianthus even though we're in the perennial chapter. Many dianthus are true perennials (although not very long-lived), among which I have never found a true red. There are some tallish named varieties, such as 'Desmond' and 'Ian', that are fine dark crimson, but they've not been perennial for me. No doubt they are for gardeners elsewhere.

There's now a new breed of dianthus that I haven't yet grown. It was created by crossing *D. chinensis* with *D. barbatus* (sweet william). Since the latter is biennial and the former annual, hardiness is not indicated. Two of the several series of these hybrids that are offered are 'Telstar' and 'Ideal'. Plants bearing the first name are purportedly proper biennials in the South, tender biennials in the North.

Plants in the 'Ideal' series are said to be true biennials from zone 2 to zone 11, as well as being more tolerant of heat. I'd like to try a few colors from each series: 'Telstar' scarlet and purple, 'Ideal' crimson and deep violet, perhaps. I wouldn't expect them to last long, but they might be good colors for the new garden. If not, they'll go in the front of the border. 'Telstar' is eight inches tall, and 'Ideal' is ten.

Dianthus are a pleasure to raise from seed; they pop up in just a few days, like radishes. It always amazes me that anything so elegant as dianthus can be so enthusiastic and cooperative. In my experience, most fancy plants have to be wheedled into germinating. I don't suppose these hybrids are fragrant, since fragrance is not mentioned. For that delicious scent you can raise some perennials, such as *D. gratianopolitanus* (cheddar pinks) or *D. plumarius* (cottage pinks), for your pastel border. They won't bloom all summer as the hybrids we've been discussing do, but their scent is heavenly and their blue-gray foliage is a great addition to any garden. I like dianthus especially in November, when the low, mat-forming species look tight and bristly, like blue hedgehogs.

PLANT LIST: PERENNIALS

1 *Achillea* 'Coronation Gold', *A. filipendulina*, *A. f.* 'Gold Plate'
2 *Alcea rosea* (hollyhock) 'Chater's Scarlet', 'Nigra'
3 *Asclepias tuberosa*, *A. curassavica*
4 *Belamcanda chinensis*, *B. flabellata*
5 *Chrysanthemum x morifolium* (*dendranthema*) 'Drummer Boy', 'Artisan', 'Happy Face', 'Flaming Sun', 'Fireside', 'Vampire'
6 *Coreopsis auriculata* 'Nana', *C. verticillata* 'Golden Showers', 'Zagreb', *C. grandiflora* 'Sunray', 'Early Sunrise', 'Goldfink', *C. lanceolata*
7 *Dianthus* 'Ideal' and 'Telstar' strains
8 *Euphorbia griffithii* 'Fireglow'
9 *Gaillardia x grandiflora* 'Burgundy', 'Goblin', 'Baby Cole', 'Kobold'
10 *Helenium autumnale* 'Butterpat', 'Kugelsonne', Zimbelsterne', 'Waldtraut', 'Crimson Beauty', 'Dunkel Pracht'
11 *Helianthus atrorubens* 'The Monarch', *H. multiflorus* 'Flore Pleno', *H. m.* 'Loddon Gold'
12 *Heliopsis helianthoides* 'Summer Sun', 'Golden Greenheart', 'Golden Plume', 'Ballerina'
13 *Hemerocallis* 'Candilla', 'Chicago Sunrise', 'Stella d'Oro', 'Red Rim', 'Carey Quinn', 'Latin Lover', 'Ed Murray'
14 *Hibiscus* 'Lord Baltimore', 'Disco Belle', *H. coccineus*
15 *Imperata cylindrica* 'Red Baron' (Japanese blood grass)
16 *Iris ensata* (Japanese) 'Dark Drapery' and others
17 *Iris sibirica* 'Caesar's Brother', 'Ruffled Velvet', 'Tealwood'
18 *Kniphofia* 'Shenandoah', 'Royal Standard'
19 *Lobelia cardinalis* and cultivars
20 *Lychnis x arkwrightii* 'Vesuvius', *L. chalcedonica* (Maltese cross)
21 *Miscanthus sinensis* var. *purpurascens*

22 *Monarda didyma* 'Cambridge Scarlet', 'Gardenview Scarlet', 'Prairie Night', 'Mahogany'

23 *Ophiopogon planiscapus* 'Nigrescens' (black mondo grass)

24 *Panicum virgatum* 'Rotstrahl-Busch', 'Haense Herms'

25 *Papaver bracteatum*

26 *Papaver orientale, P. o.* 'Beauty of Livermore', 'Bonfire', 'Allegro'

27 *Pennisetum setaceum* 'Atrosanguineum'

28 *Penstemon barbatus* 'Torre'

29 *Rudbeckia fulgida sullivantii* 'Goldsturm'

4

COOLING IT DOWN

hile considering plants for the hot garden, I looked for some that would lower the temperature here and there, and make quiet spots where the eye could rest. The first year I tried a few true blues and whites but subsequently decided that they looked absolutely irrelevant. Pure blue didn't work because it contained no red and because it contrasted with the oranges and yellows, thus spoiling the color scheme of this particular garden. White was unsuccessful as a cooler because, while theoretically containing all the colors, it serves in the garden to separate them instead of holding them together. (This color scheme seems to require close connections. I've noticed that in spring, if yellow and red flowers are blooming, they don't look really good together until the oranges come along, making the bridge, as it were.)

I finally chose for cooling purposes two kinds of purple: real Crayola purple, made by combining red and blue, as found in *Campanula glomerata;* and the purple of "purple" foliage, which is really burgundy, chianti, mahogany, and dregs-of-wine (the result of combining red and black or red and brown). These colors worked because they both contain red.

There are various versions of "purple" foliage, all of them excellent for a hot-color garden. It is important, however, to learn which plants change their purple color to green during the summer. My *Lysimachia ciliata* 'Atropurpurea' is ruby red in May and June, but as it grows taller it grows greener. *Penstemon* 'Husker's Red' changes its lovely, smooth, wine-colored spring leaves to green with red under-tones as the summer wears on. Nor does *Clematis recta* 'Purpurea' remain constant— at least not the form I have. You might be able to find a better one. Some dahlias have fine, true, dependable purple foliage (*D.* 'Ellen Houston', 'Bishop of Llandaff', 'Japanese Bishop', etc.), as do several heucheras—not only the popular 'Palace Purple' but also newer cultivars, including 'Chocolate Ruffles', 'Montrose Ruby', 'Bressing-ham Bronze', and 'Molly Bush'. There is now more than one kind of opal basil and perilla. The ribbed, smoky, brown-red leaves of the original ordinary perilla (*P. frutescens* var. *crispa*) are stunning as a background for the satin blossoms of chocolate cosmos (*Cosmos atrosanguineus*) and for all the red and orange flowers as well. Perillas do have the nasty habit of seeding themselves frantically into every crack and crevice and into the centers of the perennials. I try to cut off their heads as they are preparing to procreate, but they always manage to beat me at that game. Another fault of perillas is that of turning green as they flower and make seed. I keep cutting them back, but they are so determined that they eventually have to be pulled up and chucked over the fence.

Three kinds of "purple" cool down the fiery red-orange of Dahlia 'Ellen Houston': the bronze foliage of the dahlia itself, the corrugated chianti-colored leaves of perilla, and the real purple of Salvia 'Victoria'.

I would not chuck *Anthriscus sylvestris* 'Raven's Wing' over the fence or anywhere else, although I'll admit that it has the same sad tendency as perilla to lose its delicious dark burgundy color as the summer approaches its end; its many-times-divided lacy leaves become a mere reddish green. Nevertheless, it's a very lovely perennial for a lightly shaded corner, which its elegant low rosette will decorate for many weeks before it sends up its tall, slender stems, topped by umbels of small, whitish, undistinguished flowers.

Last spring I grew lots of purple orach (*Atriplex hortensis* 'Rubra'), beautiful plants that were all eaten by rabbits the night after I set them out. I'll try again after

***P**erilla serves to enrich yellows as well as reds. The zinnia is 'Orange Pinwheel'.*

*T*he *deep, almost sinister tones of beautiful* Ipomoea 'Blackie' *dramatize the red of* Verbena canadensis. Cuphea ignea *picks up the red farther back, and the whole group is further enlivened by the yellow daisies of a silver-foliaged perennial wildflower from the Southwest,* Melampodium cinereum.

I've installed wire netting around the garden fence. I can hardly blame the rabbits for eating it; it's delicious either raw, in salads, or slightly cooked in a little good olive oil, like spinach. The handsome plants grow five or six feet tall, in late summer, and carry large clusters of extremely decorative plummy red seeds.

Ipomoea batatas 'Blackie', the sweet potato vine, is a knockout, with eight-inch-wide, very dark, palmate leaves, and is unquestionably worth the bother it causes by not being hardy. Mine wintered over, not very happily but successfully, in a pot in the bay window in the parlor. Now it's luxuriating in the hot summer sun. I have just learned from Nancy Goodwin that I should take cuttings, which root easily, instead of digging it up.*

If our winters here were a bit milder, I'd send for *Vitis vinifera* 'Purpurea'. It's a purple-leaved vine whose praises have been sung by various horticultural experts. The six-inch, glossy, lobed leaves are ruby-colored when young, red mixed with burnt umber later. One of its common names is claret vine. It does sound somewhat alarming ("vigorous to thirty feet"), but then, grape vines are pruned severely and thrive on the treatment. No mention is made of this vine's bearing fruit. Here, on the hills around the Finger Lakes, *Vitis vinifera*, which is an old European plant, is grown in rows and rows and produces fine white wines. Maybe, since the species prospers here, I shouldn't allow myself to be daunted by the "zone 6" in the catalog and should take a chance on its being hardier than it's said to be. It would be most convenient to have a purple-leaved vine from which I needn't take cuttings every year, as I must for ipomoea. Not that I would abandon the ipomoea . . .

Purple-foliaged *Hibiscus acetosella* 'Red Shield' will make a great five-foot herbaceous shrub when it has a chance, so should be used for background plantings, perhaps. The leaves of this stunning African native are a great part of its charm, being intricately cut and several times lobed.

You may be acquainted with the good-looking, fifteen-inch *Sedum maximum* 'Atropurpureum Honeysong'. If not, search for it and consider it as a possible resident of the new garden. It will be sure to give satisfaction since, in addition to requiring no special care, it forms a clump of gray-mahogany, three-inch leaves that look handsome from spring through fall.

Not for me but for lucky gardeners farther south is a euphorbia listed as both *E. amygdaloides* 'Rubra' and *E. a.* 'Purpurea', a twelve- to eighteen-inch evergreen—or everpurple—subject that would be a good, contributing member of a flamboyant

---

* Nancy Goodwin is a horticulturist who recently closed her Montrose Nursery.

Another combination of wine-colored foliage and red: Salvia coccinea *'Lady in Red' with the lovely leaves of* Hibiscus acetosella.

garden not for its yellow spring flowers (which are composed of colored bracts rather than petals) but for the cooling and enriching quality of its wine-red stems and lance-shaped leaves. This handsome spurge will grow in light shade or sun and prefers dry rather than wet conditions.

Another purple-leaved plant I use is *Oxalis triangularis*. Its flowers are white but unobtrusive—it's the almost black leaves that count. I grow these in wide, shallow pots that are easy to move about and set in strategic places. They seem to retain their color best in filtered light. Another advantage of putting them in pots is that the small bulbs are easier to keep track of than they would be in the ground. They have to be brought indoors over the winter.

Oxalis triangularis, *kept in pots, can be shifted about where needed, preferably in semishaded* *areas.*

Oranges, yellows, and reds are contributed by marigold 'Red Marietta', 'Sunny Red' cosmos, tiger lilies, and Coreopsis verticillata on the opposite page. An explosion of blue oat grass (Helichtotrichon sempervirens) with the imposing Sedum maximum 'Atropurpureum Honeysong'.

A houseplant that can be used outdoors in summer is *Setcreasea pallida* 'Purple Heart'. Its leaves repeat almost exactly the color of those of the oxalis. I have it combined, in a pot, with red and orange geraniums.

Again it's a question of space, but if you've got lots of it, I'd strongly advise you to think about planting several purple-leaved shrubs as background plants for your hot-colored flowers. There's more than one version of the elegant smokebush— *Cotinus coggygria* var. *purpureus*—C.c.'Velvet Cloak', 'Purple Splendor', and probably

Setcreasea pallida 'Purple Heart', usually used as a houseplant, is as trouble-free and obliging outdoors as indoors and makes another cool, purple-leaved plant to combine with hot colors.

others. The matte quality of the blunt, dark-veined leaves gives this shrub a somber quality that makes it a real presence in any garden. *Prunus x cistena* is not quite so impressive with its glossy, burgundy leaves that reflect the light, but it's very pretty indeed and seems to dramatize any flower that is seen against it.

Let's wind up this discussion of purple-foliaged plants with a brief account of the many marvelous new ajugas that are now available. I have four or five of them in the long border, where they are most effective combined with sulfur yellow and blue or with silver and pink. (That's the great thing about purple foliage—it brings out the best in either cool or hot colors.) These fancy new ajugas are not such barbarians as the species and can be easily controlled. Actually, I wish that one of them— *A. pyramidalis* 'Metallica Crispa Purpurea'—would move a little faster; it made an amusing little round rug of shiny, scrunched-up, black leaves the first summer and hasn't budged since—or barely. *A. reptans* 'Royalty', on the other hand, is energetically spreading its mat of glossy, scalloped, ruffled leaves. 'Purple Brocade' is interestingly crinkled and textured, but best of all is 'Jungle Beauty Improved', whose large, rounded, wavy, maroon leaves must be nearly ten inches in diameter. A rosette of this striking plant here and there—say, next to orange calendulas, vermilion cosmos, or clear red geraniums—would be most attractive.

I have an idea that so-called black flowers would go wonderfully well with all these plants named 'Bonfire', 'Vesuvius', 'Flame', and the like. Most of us have, at one time or another, grown the annual *Centaurea cyanus*, known familiarly as bachelor's button or cornflower, and know that this fringed ray flower comes in several pretty colors, including one of the best blues to be found anywhere. Considering this fact, it seems almost criminal to contemplate growing a dark, doubled version called 'Black Ball'. It is, however, a fine feathery plant, standing about three feet high, carrying countless round, one-inch, double blossoms that are the color of cordovan or the dark leaves of the red oak in autumn. Worth growing, even by would-be purists who feel guilty when they stray from the path.

Have you ever seen what they call "black hollyhocks"? We mentioned them briefly in chapter 3—*Alcea rosea* 'Nigra'. They would stand five feet tall in the back of your garden, displaying large, silky, single blossoms of bitter-chocolate-maroon petals that grow almost black toward the center. They begin to bloom in July and would make a sumptuous background for the red-orange *Dahlia* 'Ellen Houston' and a clump or two of *Heliopsis* 'Golden Plume' or flaming daylilies. Then, this side of those plants could be some *Centaurea* 'Black Ball', mingled with single marigolds or zinnias. If you intend to grow hollyhocks from seed, be sure to set them out in holding beds for the first year, for while some of them might bloom the first year, most will wait until the second.

Hollyhocks do cross-pollinate, so if you have scarlet and black hollyhocks in the same garden, you'll have to gather the seed before it falls or, in any case, not allow the seedlings to take up residence before you've tested them in a holding garden for color.

Here I must rhapsodize a bit more about chocolate cosmos. If you haven't already tried them you must, and not just as oddities, for they are that—they have not only the color and sheen of warm chocolate but the scent as well—but for their beauty. The flowers rise on slender stems above delicate, pinnately cut foliage to a

The pelargonium on the right (name unknown) is particularly welcome because of its dark red-green leaves.

height of about eighteen inches. The petals of the two-inch ray flowers are of the richest satin in texture, and their color is a blend of burgundy and burnt umber—dark, gleaming red-brown.

I've had trouble carrying them through the winter. These are tender tuberous plants, hardy only through zone 6 (but since purveyors say zone 6 "with protection," I'll bet it's really zone 7). They come from Mexico, so you can imagine how they feel about upstate New York. Hence I dug the tubers with the dahlias and, treating them similarly, as instructed, hoped for the best. But when I had planted the perfectly healthy-looking tubers the following spring, that was the last I saw of them—they never emerged. Next winter, if I haven't found a chocolate cosmos expert by then, I'll try potting them up and putting them in a sunny window. Maybe my dark, cold basement took away all their Latin joie de vivre.

Green foliage with dark purple undertones belongs to *Dianthus barbatus* 'Dunnet's Dark Crimson', whose flowers range from crimson to dark burgundy—very nearly black. These are quite the handsomest sweet williams you can imagine, and their flowers, which start in spring, go on for many weeks. Furthermore, I have plants that have lived through two winters and are still going strong, behaving so far more like perennials than biennials, which is all they claim to be. Last spring I planted seeds of *D. b.* 'Darkest Red', whose first-year plants are already enormous, vigorous-looking specimens. This coming May I'll be able to compare the two strains.

A big problem is that of finding real purple flowers to set among the summer bloomers. In the spring there's *Campanula glomerata* 'Superba' and red-violet *C. latifolia* 'Macrantha'. But when they're gone, I've had to rely on purple Siberian and Japanese iris, while they last, and on *Veronica* 'Goodness Grows' and 'Blue Fox', neither of which is really dark enough. Nor is 'Sunny Border Blue'—at least the version of it that was sent me last year. It seems to me that 'Blue Peter', formerly in my border, was darker than any of these. And that splendid subject 'Foerster's Blue' that never stops blooming. Who sells it now? Only a wholesale nursery, apparently.

And who sells 'Romily Purple', I wonder? All summer I do have lots of *Salvia farinacea* 'Victoria' and wish that it, too, were darker.

Actually, there *is* another blue salvia whose presence is going to make a big difference in the garden next year. Last spring I bought a single specimen of *Salvia* 'Indigo Spires', not really giving serious consideration to how I was going to handle its size. Or perhaps I simply didn't believe it would grow as tall as its purveyor predicted. When it began to shoot up and out, I ran for bamboo stakes and twine. These were subsequently more or less brushed aside by the salvia, which went its own way, through and over the fence. I ended up anchoring it to a stout tithonia that was, in its turn, lashed to a post. I must say the orange and purple flowers of the two plants made a great combination, even if the staking was less than artistic. The "spires" on the salvia didn't go straight up like church spires but bent, curved, and swooped about, more like dancers than something on a building. The dark violet inflorescences reached extravagant lengths: twenty inches and more. At summer's end I took lots of cuttings, which now, late in November, are already indicating that they need to be put into pots. What if they hit the ceiling in the bay window before spring comes? It's a bit worrying, but if they and I make it through the winter they'll be pretty impressive in the garden next summer. This time I'll take firm measures from the start to stake them properly and unobtrusively. I'm planning, too, to dry some of the flowers for a winter bouquet; when twenty degrees were predicted last October, I cut all the blossoms off my one plant and put them into a bucket of water on the (enclosed) back porch. They made a gorgeous mass of color for weeks and finally dried all by themselves, although their stems were still in the water.

Salvia 'Purple Majesty', bought and planted at the same time as 'Indigo Spires', didn't work out so well, probably because it was wanting something it wasn't getting. It kept growing but making only leaves for a long time. Then it moped, drooped, and discarded a branch here and there. Finally, shortly before the first frost, it took heart—began to put forth healthy leaves and handsome, long, blackish-purple flowers. But by then it was too late. I was too cross with it to take cuttings.

The annual heliotrope called 'Marine' is a perfect purple, but I have the deuce of a time germinating the seed, due to my cold house, perhaps.

Ah, but last spring in our local garden/hardware store I found a flat of the richest dark velvet petunias I've ever seen. They're quite large but single and are called 'Midnight Dreams'. Their color repeats, with interest, that of the lustrous purple clematis on the fence.

I would have *Buddleia* 'Nanho Purple' or 'Black Knight' if only they would live through the winter.

Pansies come in the right shades of purple, but they wouldn't like the heat in my garden. No more would *Delphinium* 'Black Knight', I imagine, but that is no reason other gardeners could not use it. It's the only delphinium of a suitable color, coming as it does in shades of dark violet and having a black, rather than white, bee.

If you're already a whiz at growing delphinium, you won't have to be told that the double ones require serious staking (and in good time, before they get too tall) and that they may be troubled with cyclamen mites and mildew, depending on your climate and soil. I'm told that people in Colorado have no trouble growing delphinium, and I saw them in Frank Cabot's garden in Quebec, as stout as cabbages, flourishing and free of afflictions.

I always prepare the spot before planting them by digging in lots of old cow manure and agricultural lime. Each spring and fall I serve them with more of the same.

Dark purple Japanese iris (*Iris ensata*) and Siberian iris (*I. sibirica*—see chapter 3)—will furnish you with more cool spots and will appreciate peat and sulfur (or some acid fertilizer) along with the manure you'll work in before planting them. Cottonseed meal, generously applied, is a fine fertilizer for calcifuge plants, by the way (it put new life into my heathers that had been thoroughly disheartened by an especially grim winter). These iris also benefit from the application of a fluffy, nourishing mulch. I get old silage from a nearby dairy farmer and find it to be the perfect mulch for perennials: it is fine, dark, lightweight, and, unlike wood chips, it feeds the plants as it becomes incorporated into the soil instead of taking nitrogen away from them. However, lacking silage, gardeners can no doubt find good commercial mulches that are not—repeat not—chips or chopped bark.

One more good purple perennial is *Monarda* 'Prairie Night', also mentioned in chapter 3. Monardas are especially valuable because they are so long-blooming and because even when their glory days are over for the year they retain a certain charm, like that of a lady who grows old gracefully.

PLANT LIST: COOLING IT DOWN

Plants with purple or mahogany flowers

1   *Alcea rosea* 'Nigra'
2   *Buddleia* 'Nanho Purple', 'Black Knight'
3   *Campanula glomerata* 'Superba', 'Joan Elliott', *C. latifolia* 'Macrantha'
4   *Centaurea cyanus* 'Black Ball'
5   *Cosmos atrosanguineus*
6   *Dahlia* 'Rep City', 'Crossfield Ebony', 'Envy' (see chapter 6)
7   *Delphinium* 'Black Knight'
8   *Dianthus barbatus* 'Dunnet's Dark Crimson', 'Darkest Red'
9   *Heliotropium* 'Marine'
10 *Iris ensata, I. sibirica*
11 *Monarda* 'Prairie Night'
12 *Petunia* 'Midnight Dreams', 'Primetime Blue', and others

13 *Salvia farinacea* 'Victoria', *S.* 'Indigo Spires'

14 *Veronica* 'Goodness Grows', 'Sunny Border Blue', 'Blue Peter', 'Foerster's Blue'

Plants with "purple" foliage

1 *Ajuga pyramidalis* 'Metallica Crispa Purpurea', *A. reptans* 'Royalty', 'Purple Brocade', 'Jungle Beauty Improved'

2 *Anthriscus sylvestris* 'Raven's Wing'

3 *Atriplex hortensis* 'Rubra'

4 *Cotinus coggygria* (see also chapter 5)

5 *Dahlia* 'Ellen Houston', 'Bishop of Llandaff', 'Japanese Bishop'

6 *Euphorbia amygdaloides* 'Rubra' ('Purpurea')

7 *Heuchera* 'Palace Purple', 'Montrose Ruby', 'Chocolate Ruffles', and others

8 *Hibiscus acetosella* 'Red Shield'

9 *Ipomoea batatas* 'Blackie'

10 *Ocimum basilicum* 'Purple Ruffles' (basil)

11 *Ophiopogon planiscapus* 'Nigrescens'

12 *Oxalis triangularis*

13 *Perilla frutescens* var. *crispa*

14 *Prunus x cistena* (see also chapter 5)

15 *Sedum maximum* 'Atropurpureum Honeysong'

16 *Setcreasea pallida* 'Purple Heart'

17 *Vitis vinifera* 'Purpurea'

5

VINES AND SHRUBS

oom should certainly be found in the kind of garden we are discussing for shrubs and vines, especially the latter, if the garden is, like mine, enclosed within a fence. *Vitis vinifera* 'Purpurea' and *Ipomoea* 'Blackie', mentioned in chapter 4, will decorate part of the fence, and one is certainly grateful to clematis for gracefully clothing many other parts of the plain cedar boards, as well as contributing the exact shades of purple that are needed. So far I've planted *Clematis x jackmanii*, C. 'The President', 'Lady Betty Balfour', and 'Polish Spirit'. (I did have the satiny, plum-red 'Niobe' but lost it during the frightful winter of 1993–94.) They all bloom elegantly and profusely over a long period. In fact, they're so successful that I plan to add several more. 'Lord Nevill' is another plum that might be tougher than 'Niobe'. A large, late-

blooming purple, 'Gypsy Queen', sounds alluring. Maybe those two and another *jackmanii* will do, but it's hard not to be greedy. I don't use the yellow *C. tangutica*, considering it too pale for this garden.

The same winter (1993–94) did in *Lonicera brownii* 'Dropmore Scarlet' as well as the clematis (the lonicera is listed for zones 3–9), leaving me with only one other, an apparently more valiant honeysuckle, *L. heckrottii*, whose pretty pink-and-yellow flowers nourish the hummingbirds, who don't hold it against them, as I do, that they're not really bright enough for the garden.

The trouble with writing about plants is that it sets you prowling through catalogs to see whether the plant you're talking about is still being sold. And the trouble with *that* is that you discover more plants you simply must have, no matter what. I've just come upon *Lonicera japonica* 'Purpurea', which is described as having "purplish-red" flowers (could the writer mean magenta?). And another one, *L. sempervirens* 'Cedar Lane' with "deep red tubular blooms." If only they are tough, and as nice as they sound!

Trumpet vines (*Campsis radicans*) are growing over, under, and through the fence but are stubbornly refusing to flower. Why so, for heaven's sake? If campsis finds our winters too cold, why doesn't it simply and straightforwardly *die* instead of hanging around making lots of leaves and miles of vine but no orange trumpets? And if it's the cold that ails it, why is it, too, listed in all catalogs and reference books as being suitable for zones 4–9?

If trumpet vine does well in your part of the country and you have fences or pergolas on which it can clamber (which it will do quite expertly, requiring guidance, rather than assistance, from you), why not get several? Or a couple, at least.

See how cleverly the Japanese iris brings the color of the clematis (Clematis x jackmanii) on the fence to the foreground. The tithonia, now standing demurely behind the rudbeckia, is just getting ready to push all its neighbors aside—or under.

Here I am, cheerfully advising you to plant two vines that can travel thirty or forty feet, either up or along the ground! But with a good pair of pruning shears and a stout lopper you should be able, if you are fast on your feet, to keep them from taking over the property. C. radicans 'Flava', although a lovely plant, looks to be too soft a yellow for our purposes, but 'Crimson Trumpet', in pure glowing red, would be splendid. C. grandiflora, Chinese trumpet vine, is more tender (zone 7) than the American radicans and has larger scarlet funnels. The showy three-inch flowers appear in August. C. x tagliabuana is a cross between the two plants, Chinese and American, and would presumably be less hardy than radicans. However, a red cultivar, C. x t. 'Mme. Galen', is listed in one catalog at least for zones 5–9. I'd be a bit skeptical. Zone 6, maybe? This spectacular hybrid is named for its breeders, the Tagliabue brothers, who ran a nursery near Milan some years back. French nursery-men subsequently bred various cultivars from it. 'Mme. Galen', the best-known cultivar, appeared in 1889. And I found all this out from Michael Dirr's Manual of Woody Landscape Plants, which should be in your garden book library if it isn't.*

Trumpet vines climb by means of rootlike holdfasts and are consequently very good at scaling walls and fences. The only problem is, they get so carried away with the urge to go onward and upward that they fail to think of the future and to dis-tribute their weight safely, thus often becoming so heavy on top that their handfasts can't keep them anchored through bad windstorms. You'll have to think for them. That seems to be the only hazard, for campsis appear to be insect- and disease-free.

If your garden is large and you have the courage to cope with another ram-bunctious shrub/vine, you can include bittersweet—either the American native, Celastrus scandens, or the Chinese species, C. orbiculatus, which is now becoming naturalized in parts of the eastern United States. With any luck, bittersweet fruit would pick up and repeat some of the colors of the late-blooming chrysanthemums

---

* Rev. ed. (Champaign, Ill.: Stipes Publishing Company, 1990).

and heleniums. I've seen the native vine pruned so as to make neat shrubs, but you could, if you prefer, train it against a wall or fence. You could also use the dried berries in a winter bouquet, along with some of your *Gomphrena* 'Strawberry Fayre', which is an orange, not strawberry, red.

While we're on the subject of colorful fruit, I want to suggest that spacious hot-color gardens could include pyracantha, grown either as a shrub or espaliered against a fence or wall. Some pyracanthas will carry masses of orange or red berries from August into winter, if the birds don't devour them. A well-grown shrub is a splendid sight indeed; I only wish our winters weren't quite so cold. Most of the varieties so far available are listed for zones 6, 7, and 8, although some claim zone 5 for 'Mojave'. We had, in Virginia, a glorious unnamed specimen that clambered up an outside brick chimney to the roof, but I haven't planted it here. Mr. Dirr says "the hardiest types will probably be killed at around −20 degrees F" (p. 676). The genus *is* susceptible to various diseases—scab and fire blight among them—although disease-resistant types are now on the market.

A year or so ago, after a long and bitter relationship with an ancient wisteria that grew against the back of our house, I fell upon it with instruments of destruction—shovel, saw, lopping shears, and pickax—and, after the battle was over, replaced it with a row of demure and docile spireas. The strife between the wisteria and me had arisen from the fact that I am not a good pruner, tending as I do to simply hack at branches that get in my way rather than scientifically and artistically shaping the subject. So I had felt more and more helpless as the old vine, knowing all the tricks, took advantage of me. It would race madly around to the front of the house, behind and under the Korean lilacs, rooting as it ran. It wiggled its way under the clapboard siding of the house and even into the basement. Outdoors it sent long tendrils out to catch in the hair of passersby. When it took to climbing into my bedroom around the window screen, I decided I'd had enough and demolished it. Not that the wisteria considers itself dead; it surges blithely up from its grave under the spireas, waving its lovely new apricot-tinted leaves about so beguilingly that I feel like a brute as I cut them down. I suppose this will go on forever unless I resort to Roundup. But listen to this: There's a new problem. I've just seen, in a nursery plant list, a double *dark violet-purple* wisteria—*W. sinensis* 'Black Dragon'. Good grief, I say to myself, is this going to start all over again?

As for ordinary shrubs—the kind that just sit there instead of running about—there are several that are well adapted to fulfill our requirements.

I have *Potentilla* 'Gold Star' on one side of my garden, where it covers itself with bright yellow, well-shaped blossoms all summer long. There are many shrubby potentillas in several colors, but if you're thinking of getting some for a hot-color garden, be sure to look for those with blooms of a strong yellow. The old *P. fruticosa* 'Sutter's Gold' is one of these, but there are newer ones: 'Hollandia Gold', with large, deep yellow flowers; 'Goldfinger', a spreading shrub of two to three feet in height. Everblooming 'Gold Drop' remains at two feet and is more compact. Canada has launched what must be the first potentilla to bear double and semidouble blossoms. Its breeders have named it 'Yellowbird', and I'm coveting it.

If you don't own them, you've probably seen pictures of *Potentilla* 'Tangerine' and 'Red Ace', both from England, I believe. I've not ordered them myself, because I read that while they are truly coppery red in cool weather, they turn yellow in heat or full (broiling) sun. I should think, then, that they'd be most satisfactory in gardens in Washington State and northwestern Oregon. There is no reason, though, why gardeners in the northeastern and central states shouldn't try them in part shade.

Potentillas are very easy to please and accept with equanimity almost any amount of cutting back, which is often necessary to keep them from draping their branches over their close neighbors.

Across the central path from the potentilla is a real princess of a shrub: *Hypericum frondosum*. Part of the attraction of this little bush is its small, blue-green, oppo-

Monarda *'Blue Stocking'*, *not knowing that its days in this garden are numbered, is looking very comfortable behind* Potentilla *'Gold Star'*. *One 'Bishop of Llandaff' dahlia blossom is trying to rise up under the honeysuckle,* Lonicera heckrottii.

---

site leaves, but the flowers that appear from late June to mid-August (larger than those of most other hypericums) remind me of the striated, real twenty-four-karat gold haloes that Fra Angelico gave to his saints and angels. Up from the center of each yellow blossom spring thick, soft whisks of gleaming gold stamens—quite lovely and somehow ethereal. These eventually turn into plump, pointed fruits (the shape of Hershey's chocolate Kisses), each surrounded by a ruff of small, green leaves.

Anyone driving in spring or summer through southern Europe, the Middle East, or North Africa, winding through the hills while traveling from town to town, will be gladdened by the sight of foaming masses of yellow broom, cascading over rocks or lying in low, prostrate mounds. These are various species of cytisus, genista, and spartium—all members of the pea family, as is easily seen by an examination of their flowers. Many of these species (and their cultivars) are used in gardens, especially in Britain and on the continent, but more frequently now than formerly in this country. They make splendid additions to the garden. All three genera are available from American nurseries, but since spartium will survive only in zone 8 we will deal here with the genista and cytisus. Generally speaking, genistas are hardier than cytisus and they have blooms of strong yellow, whereas those of cytisus can be deep or pale yellow, as well as white, red, and lavender. All of the brooms want full sun, very sharp drainage, and spare soil, tending toward acid rather than alkaline. Damp, richly manured clay soil would be the death of them. Another characteristic all brooms share is that of being intolerant of disturbance; hence you must buy young potted plants and set them out where they are to remain. Many brooms have very fragrant blossoms, and all of them have slim, green branches and small leaves. Some are evergreen. In some species the leaves are so small as to be almost nonexistent, and the green stems take over the job of feeding the roots.

I've grown both cytisus and genista and have seen many others but have always wondered what the difference was between them—they look so much alike. I finally found the answer, in *The Royal Horticultural Society Dictionary of Gardening*. Just in case you, too, have been puzzled as to how the two genera differ, I quote the dictionary on cytisus:

The seeds show a wart-like eminence, the strophiole, near the hilum; it represents the seed-end of the finicle; i.e. the cord which ties the seed to the pod. Presence of the strophiole is the only reliable means of distinguishing cytisus from genista.*

* (Oxford: Clarendon Press, 1994), vol. 2, p. 624.

No wonder I had trouble telling them apart. I was somewhat distressed to find the RHS writer declaring that the synonym for *Cytisus decumbens* is *Genista prostrata* or *Spartium decumbens*. The synonym for *C. ardoninii* is *G. ardoninii* . . . and so on . . . Goodness! If genista can be a synonym for cytisus, to say nothing of spartium, why not quit worrying about the strophiole, roll them all into one genus, and simplify our lives?

If you live in zone 6 or farther south or, it goes without saying, in the Pacific Northwest, you'll be able to grow many of the cytisus, starting with *C. decumbens*, a three- to four-foot shrub with bright, shiny, deep yellow flowers. The only trouble will be that it, like many brooms, blooms only in spring; but, depending on the size and design of your garden, you could use it with red and orange tulips and/or other early flowers with fiery colors. Six-foot Scotch broom (*C. scoparius*), also a spring-flowering plant, is another candidate, and one of its cultivars, *C. s.* 'Burkwoodii', has garnet-red flowers with yellow margins. Then there's *C. x praecox* 'Allgold', slightly smaller at five feet. A fourteen-inch hybrid, *C. x beanii*, is hardier than most cytisus. It's said to survive in zone 5 and, since it, too, has chrome yellow flowers, would be tempting to northerners who would like a little decumbent shrub. *C. nigricans*, however, often blooms all summer, which would suit our purposes better. If it does stop blooming in summer, this three- to five-foot shrub reblooms in the fall. The flowers are yellow, and Mr. Wyman says it's for zone 5. But then, he says *C. x praecox* is for zone 5, and I lost it in its third winter. Admittedly, it could have been due to my clay soil and insufficient drainage.

Safer for cold climates are several genista species, especially *tinctoria*, which is hardy through zone 4. (Wyman says zone 2.) I have a dear little prostrate version of it with tiny, dark green leaves and bright yellow, double flowers, *G. t.* 'Flore Pleno'. It blooms in summer rather than spring, which is an added advantage. Plain *G. tinctoria* reaches a height of eighteen to thirty inches, if you want a taller shrub, but *G. t.* 'Royal Gold' produces, according to its purveyors, a greater quantity of brighter flowers. For zone 5 there is 'Winged Broom', a low, spreading subject with curious winged branches, G. *sagittalis* by name; also G. *pilosa*, a dwarf ground cover that blooms in spring in my garden; and G. *p.* 'Vancouver Gold', which will form undulating, dark green mounds. Yellow flowers, of course. Farther south (zone 7) you can grow, among other species, dwarf G. *lydia* or fifteen- to twenty-inch G. *aethnensis*, the Mt. Etna broom, which, happily, blooms in midsummer.

By the way, did you know that the Plantagenets got their name from genista (French *genêt*), a branchlet of which they wore as a family emblem?

Kerria is a perfect color—the double one, that is: *Kerria japonica* 'Pleniflora', a shrub that breaks out in deep yellow pom-poms in spring, all down its dark green, slender, arching branches. This is definitely not a compact shrub; it grows up and up, to about six feet, then drapes itself over and down. I'm very fond of the smaller, single, variegated kerria, but its blossoms are the color of whipped butter—much too subdued for this garden.

There are roses that would be splendid in a garden that has room for them. I'm not sure that hybrid teas would do, although some of them, such as 'Cary Grant' and 'Dolly Parton', come in orange, and some ('Ink Spots' and 'Black Garnet') in very dark red. These are the right colors, but, even if one could forgive the breeders for creating an orange rose and even if the black-red ones were very beautiful, do you think that such formal, such elegant roses belong in a jungle? They might look out of place, as my friend said of the astilbes.

I do think that if roses are to be tried in this kind of garden, they should be either as informal as the old climber 'Blaze' (which British garden writers have had so much fun deriding) or those in the category usually designated as "landscape roses." Their blossoms are small and not so opulent as those of hybrid teas, and are borne in clusters so that they look more like wild roses. Two that I've found are both Meidiland. The first, 'Sevillana' (Meigehnir), is a shrub measuring three and a half to five feet by two and a half to three feet. It is *said* to bloom from spring until frost with clusters of brilliant red, double roses that, furthermore, produce scarlet fruit in autumn. "Pest and disease-resistant." Sounds almost too good to be true.

Another one, 'Scarlet Meidiland' (Meikrotal), seems to be the right color but may be better for holding a bank than it would be for a place in our new garden, since, although it grows up to no more than three or four feet, it sprawls out to a width of five to six feet. If you enjoy putting on a suit of armor and cutting back roses, you might like to take this one on, but I confess to not having the courage myself. I've become, with the passage of time, less and less tolerant of plants that strike back savagely when one tries to minister to their needs. When I've finished the spring pruning and weeding of the border roses, I look as punctured and torn as Jesus in the Grünevald triptych, and I turn with relief to deal with plants that are quietly grateful for one's attentions. Still . . . 'Sevillana' looks mighty tempting . . .

Some quite gorgeous nonlandscape roses could probably be used where there is lots of space in the sun. A six- to eight-foot shrub with dark green foliage is *Rosa x kordesii* 'Dortmund', particularly striking for being single, thus displaying its gold stamens. Kordes hybrids are said to be especially resistant to disease.

So is the yellow floribunda 'Sun Sprite', but you must remember—or realize, if you haven't grown them before—that most roses in most parts of the United States require a lot of spraying if they are to flourish and maintain a respectable appearance all summer. A few of my border roses ('New Dawn', 'Ballerina', 'The Fairy', *Rosa spinosissima* 'Alba Plena', *R. pimpinellifolia* 'Double White') are absolutely disease-free, but others, including a lovely hybrid, 'Frühlingsgold', one of whose parents is *spinosissima*, have lost all their leaves by late summer. Rugosas, in which I invested heavily, having been told they had no problems, started losing whole canes, which I had to cut off all through the summer. I finally had enough of that exercise and dug them all up—with great regret, especially when saying good-bye to 'Thérèse Bugnet' and 'Blanc Double de Coubert'. Spraying was bad enough when it was simply a disagreeable task, but now, when the job is accompanied by feelings of

guilt, I try to avoid it by not growing plants I know will need poison to get them through the season.

We were talking about warm autumn color, as produced by bittersweet, pyracantha, heleniums, and chrysanthemums, but didn't mention hollies, hydrangeas, and viburnums. Both American (*Ilex opaca*) and English (*I. aquifolium*) hollies can be used, depending on where you live. (The shiny English holly is somewhat tender.) Or you can opt for those wonderful hybrids developed by Kathleen Meserve of Long Island, New York, which will survive in zone 5. 'Blue Boy', 'Blue Girl', and other cultivars of *Ilex x meserveae* have blue-green leaves that are as glossy as those of English holly and will bear lots of red berries if you'll set male and female plants not too far apart. A less fancy holly, the American *Ilex verticillata,* would also give you a fine display of scarlet fruit in autumn. Do you know this midheight deciduous shrub? One can find it here in the Northeast, clustered in large colonies, around the edges of ponds, where it makes splendid splashes of color. I grew lots of them from seed I gathered one winter. As you might surmise, they do best where they have a good supply of water, but they can make do with less. Of course there are plenty of special named selections that are no doubt more colorful, even, than mine, although it's hard to imagine.

As to viburnums, many of them have red leaves and/or red fruit, but many are too big to be considered eligible for this project. (I have a *Viburnum opulus* that is almost obscuring the view of a huge barn out back.) It's true there is a smaller, more civilized version of this species—*V. o. 'Compactum'*—that reaches only five feet in height and width. Sounds more manageable. The species lolls about, rooting at the nodes and eventually forming a large, tangled *V. opulus* plantation. Japanese *Viburnum wrightii* will attain eight feet but is quite compact and upright. Its red

---

Is there a redder rose than **Rosa x kordesii 'Dortmund'?**

Spacious hot-color gardens can include shrubs that will provide autumn color. Foremost among them is the northern native holly, Ilex verticillata, *sometimes called winterberry.*

berries are particularly attractive: dark red, long, and solid. *V. setigerum* (tea viburnum), though, might be your best choice, for although it can, under favorable conditions, form a ten-by-eight-foot shrub, it doesn't sprawl and is an arresting sight all season—first because of its long, pointed leaves that are purple-toned with a metallic sheen in spring, then dark green in summer, changing to persimmon in the fall; second, it produces its large clusters of scarlet fruit prolifically. *V. setigerum* is often listed as being hardy through zone 5, but it died here the second winter, in spite of having been placed in one of the warmer corners of my old garden. *V. wrightii* survives.

The oak-leaved hydrangea (*H. quercifolia*) will furnish fine fall color and is a remarkably good-looking shrub all summer. In the cold north country it will freeze

A *tea viburnum (Viburnum setigerum 'Aurantiacum') is hung with bright fruit to accompany its red autumn leaves.*

Whoever designed this planting was thinking ahead to fall color when placing a Gomphrena 'Strawberry Fayre' next to an oak leaf hydrangea.*

to the ground in winter, so will not flower, but that would be all the better for a hot garden, where the red autumn leaves are what we want.

There are scads of shrubs with yellow foliage, which you might include in your plans if yellow foliage appeals to you. Golden spireas, junipers, chamaecyparis—even elderberries—are out there waiting for you. An eight- to ten-foot shrub with beautiful, deeply cut, golden leaves, *Sambucus racemosa* 'Sutherland' is a lovely feathery thing and is not so apt to brown in the sun as a similar variety, *S. r.* 'Plumosa Aurea'.

Admittedly, this glorious golden chamaecyparis wouldn't fit in every garden.

If you get 'Sutherland', give it plenty of room in full sun. In shade its leaves will tend toward green.

As we wind up this chapter, remember the two purple-leaved shrubs we discussed in chapter 4: *Prunus x cistena* and *Cotinus coggygria* var. *purpureus*.

PLANT LIST: VINES AND SHRUBS

1 *Buddleia davidii* 'Black Knight', 'Nanho Purple' (chapter 4)
2 *Campsis grandiflora*, *C. radicans*, *C. r.* 'Crimson Trumpet', *C. x tagliabuana* 'Mme. Galen'
3 *Celastrus orbiculatus*, *C. scandens*

4   *Clematis x jackmanii*, C. 'Gypsy Queen', 'Niobe', 'The President', 'Polish Spirit', and others

5   *Cotinus coggygria* var. *purpureus*, C. c. 'Velvet Cloak', 'Purple Splendor' (see also chapter 4)

6   *Cytisus decumbens*, C. scoparius, C. s. 'Burkwoodii', C. x praecox 'Allgold'

7   *Genista pilosa, G. tinctoria, G. sagittalis, and others*

8   *Hydrangea quercifolia*

9   *Hypericum frondosum*

10   *Ilex opaca, I. aquifolium, I. verticillata, I. x meserveae* 'Blue Boy', 'Blue Girl', and others

11   *Ipomoea batatas* 'Blackie'

12   *Kerria japonica* 'Pleniflora'

13   *Lonicera brownii* 'Dropmore Scarlet', *L. sempervirens* 'Cedar Lane', *L. japonica* 'Purpurea'

14   *Potentilla fruticosa* 'Goldfinger', 'Gold Star', 'Hollandia Gold', 'Sutter's Gold', 'Red Ace', 'Yellowbird'

15   *Prunus x cistena*

16   *Pyracantha* 'Mohave' and others

17   *Rosa* 'Blaze', 'Sevillana', 'Scarlet Meidiland', 'Sun Sprite', *R. x kordesii* 'Dortmund'

18   Roses, miniature (see the list at the end of chapter 8)

19   *Sambucus racemosa* 'Sutherland'

20   *Viburnum opulus* 'Compactum', *V. wrightii, V. setigerum*

21   *Vitis vinifera* 'Purpurea'

22   *Wisteria sinensis* 'Black Dragon'

6

BULBS, CORMS,
AND TUBERS

ine additions to the hot garden are the slender, dwarf, fiery red gladioli, some of which are hardy in districts slightly warmer than mine. I'm not referring to *Gladiolus byzantinus*, which I grow in the border and which *is* hardy here, but, being magenta, is the wrong color for the new garden.

Hardy dwarf gladioli are advertised as being suitable for zones 4–9, and I humbly concede that their demise in my nursery could have been caused by horticultural ineptitude on my part. As I reread the advertisement, where their vendor swears that their corms are impervious to cold way into Canada, and that they thrive on "benign neglect," I'm almost persuaded to order the two-foot, red 'Robinetta' again. The "hardy" gladioli bloom in spring and early summer, while other dwarfs wait until late summer.

I've been growing two of these the last few years, both one and a half to two feet tall and vermilion: 'Comet' and 'Amanda Mahy'. I have not begrudged them the time it takes to dig and store them; they're neat, pretty, and really self-sufficient plants, needing no staking or spraying and giving no trouble over the winter. The corms remain plump and dry in paper bags in the basement, not causing the anxiety that dahlia tubers do.

I suppose that old hands at dealing with dahlias don't tell themselves uneasily every few weeks all winter that they'd better go down and check on the dahlias. I do that and, what's worse, keep putting it off because I don't know what to do after peering at them. If I dampen them too much, they go slimy; yet if I don't dampen them enough, they shrivel. A great worry.

Especially do I fret over the 'Bishop of Llandaff', the most beautiful of all, given me by an English friend and so far unobtainable in this country. The plant is three to five feet tall, has lovely mahogany, compound, incised leaves that are surmounted by semidouble flowers of the most vivid red imaginable, with yellow centers. They are about four inches across.

Last winter I tended the dahlia tubers pretty well, it seems, for all of them save two remained sound and have produced healthy budded or blooming plants.

'Ellen Houston' is a good one for a hot garden, growing to little more than two, sometimes three feet, its good purple foliage topped with reddish orange, semidouble blossoms. Midheight 'Japanese Bishop' (an Oriental rather than a Welsh clergy-man?) also has dark wine-colored, glossy leaves and plump blooms of luscious crimson. This year I tried some "miniature" dahlias (mine were 'Royal Simon'), plants that start to bloom at one foot and never grow higher than two. Actually, mine stayed their growth at a foot and a half. I was afraid they would look stumpy, but

---

Gladiolus *'Comet' is in full swing as* Achillea *'Coronation Gold' is winding up its summer show.*

somehow they manage to avoid it, perhaps because the plants are bushy and the flowers no more than three inches wide. They were most satisfactory and added a lot of color to the garden after the lilies and daylilies had stopped contributing. I'll tend their tubers carefully this winter and will try putting some of them in large pots next summer, as well as in the ground. It's always a good thing to have extra plants one can move into a disaster area or a spot where color is lacking due to other plants' having terminated their annual show.

When I decided to try dahlias, I ordered only midheight and short ones, partly because I wanted to avoid having to stake them. One of the reasons I had shunned them all these years was that I had a vivid memory of my Uncle Bill's garden in Chicago, which consisted of rows and rows of huge dahlias with outsize heads, each plant bound tightly to a stake—almost garroted, it seemed to me. A disturbing spectacle. So I thought to avoid altogether having to support my dahlias. But I was too sanguine. I should know by now that any herbaceous plant that has been persuaded by man to produce blossoms larger and heavier than those it originally had in mind (unless its breeder has concentrated on stems as well as flowers) doesn't even dream of shouldering the task of remaining erect. Why, indeed, should it? It's already done its bit. And so I stake—not, to be sure, using Uncle Bill's method, but my usual one of inserting three strong, slender bamboo canes around the plant *low enough so that they don't show*. I then run a strong, soft cord of gray-green around the whole bush. Naturally, this is best done before the plant flops, not after.

A word about bamboo canes. The only ones I've seen have been painted that appalling, unnatural green that cancels out all the soft, subtle greens of nature—which is why I've preferred, until recently, to use stakes cut from shrubs and trees in the woods. But now I've discovered that if you leave the commercial bamboo stakes out in the weather for a month or so, they fade to a lovely gray-green. Someone has just told me that undyed bamboo stakes are offered by at least one mail-order company.

As gardeners new to the genus browse through the dahlia catalogs, they'll find so many flowers of so many different shapes and sizes, as well as colors, that their heads will spin—cactus, semicactus, anemone, collarette, pom-pom—some of them like huge, spidery sea-creatures and some like buttons, with lots of others in between. There's a large, new black one, 'Rip City', and a tiny, black pom-pom named 'Crossfield Ebony'. 'Envy' is also red-black (Why "envy," then? Shouldn't it

Dahlia *'Border Princess'*. Monarda *'Gardenview Scarlet' stands behind it.*

be green?) There are scarlet, flame, and orange varieties in all sizes and forms—it's like a candy store. Why not get just a few, to start with? They do multiply, and if you're a northerner, you must keep in mind that they have to be dug, cleaned, and stored every fall. The space they take up on my basement floor keeps increasing.

Perhaps the most smashing individuals in a flamboyant garden will be those that come from lily bulbs. Think of tiger lilies—*Lilium lancifolium (tigrinum)*—which even have an appropriate name. (Although, come to think of it, since they have spots instead of stripes, should surely be called leopard lilies?) I've been using lilies, most of which I get from Dutch Gardens—tall orange, flame, and ruby-red ones ('Elite', 'Grand Paradiso', 'Black Beauty', and 'America') that bloom in June and early July—

Tiger lilies, cosmos, and coreopsis. Even the shiny black bulbils on the stems of the lilies serve to enliven the color combination.

An Oriental hybrid lily, 'Black Beauty', with a cultivated goldenrod from Germany, Solidago *'Goldstrahl'.*

but having seen tiger lilies in someone else's hot garden this summer, I'm now rummaging through catalogs, hot on their trail. I'm eager to have them, not only because they're so splendid with their great nodding trumpets whose orange petals curve upward to show their purple-black spots, but also because they bloom in July and August when other lilies have finished. There are several forms of tiger lilies, it seems—the common species; then *L. l. flaviflorum*, in yellow; plus one called *L. l. fortunei giganteum*, which is said to carry as many as fifty flowers on each five-foot stem. That sounds like overkill for my small garden (though perhaps not for yours), so I'm trying to find *L. l. 'Splendens'*. The authorities seem to agree that this one is the most beautiful and that it blooms the latest, in August and September. I'll see if I can get this and plain *Lilium lancifolium*, which is anything but plain.

I'm finally reading up on lily culture and intend to prepare the soil properly for the newcomers, although the directions are somewhat daunting. Digging a large area down to eighteen inches and filling it with peat and compost, then surrounding the bulbs with sand, sounds like a lot of work—but is it too much for such magnificent creatures as these? I only hope that, after such heroic measures have been taken, the lilies don't succumb to botrytis, which has decimated so many lilies in the long border.

I should add that, when I read that tiger lilies had, for over a thousand years, been raised as a food crop by people in Korea, China, and Japan, I thought that if I didn't know better, I'd have concluded that those people had no aesthetic sense whatsoever. And perhaps—who knows?—they put the flowers in a vase in the house to gaze at appreciatively as they consumed the bulbs.

'Enchantment' lilies are perfect partners for dark violet Japanese iris; they're the right color, the right height, and they bloom at the same time, at least in my garden. The fact that their clusters of glistening, orange blossoms face upward adds strength to the color combination. 'Enchantment' lilies have been around for a long time and are real troopers; rarely do they succumb to the afflictions that lilies are prone to. One can't but be grateful.

For next spring I've ordered bulbs of one- to two-foot *Lilium pumilum* (*tenuifolium*), which has fragrant, scarlet Turk's cap flowers. That is, I *hope* they're the color they're said to be, despite their common name of coral lily. They come from the East—China, Korea, Mongolia, and Siberia—so I should think they would like our climate. Their foliage is grassy and they want full sun. Many lilies want soil on the acid side, but these little things do not object to a bit of lime in the sandy soil they prefer. I plan to put the bulbs in containers as an experiment; this species is reputed to be somewhat ephemeral, but perhaps I can control their environment better in containers than in the ground, and thus prolong their lives.

Another lily—or lily relative—I'll be trying for the first time this summer is *Sprekelia formosissima* (Aztec lily), a member of the Amaryllidaceae and a genus that

One of the best and most reliable lilies, 'Enchantment'.

has but one (or some say two) species. The twelve-inch stems that bear the amazing dark crimson flowers (looking something like cockatoos) appear before the twenty-four-inch, straplike leaves. Directions for handling these bulbs are quite specialized: they are to be set with one-half to one-third of the bulb above ground and watered sparingly until growth appears. But here's the catch. According to one writer, they want full sun but need protection from *rain*. Well, here they're going to have to take what comes in the way of summer weather, willy nilly. I can't see myself erecting little shrines around them or rushing out with umbrellas every time it thunders. What happens to them in the wilds of Mexico, I wonder? Who supplies the umbrellas?

Since sprekelias are tender and want to remain undisturbed for at least three years, I'm going to plant them in pots that I can set to rest over the winter in a warm, dry place, as directed. Who knows if I will succeed with these odd strangers?

Less whimsical individuals are crocosmias, plants I first saw growing wild in our old neglected Turkish garden in Algeria. You know what they look like, don't you? They have slim, swordlike leaves similar to those of gladioli, while their funnel-shaped flowers, in shades of yellow, red, or orange (smaller than those of gladioli), crowd together, perched on the tips of arching stems. There are several species of crocosmia but the plants we use in our gardens have been developed over many years.

In the 1800s the Lemoines of France crossed two species, *Crocosmia aurea* and a somewhat hardy one, C. *pottsii*. The result, which they (regrettably) called

Crocosmia *'Lucifer' is the one most readily available in this country.*

Garden designer Lynden Miller combines Crocosmia '*Lucifer*' *with daylilies, variegated dogwood, yarrows, and dark, ruffled perilla at the New York Botanical Garden.*

C. crocosmiiflora, was not only a good plant but fertile, making it possible for other breeders to set to work producing lots of good cultivars from its seedlings. The new plants caught on in England, where British plantsmen created another series of fine cultivars with blossoms of various sizes and shades of red and gold. Many of these old French and British plants (often referred to as montbretias) have been lost, but efforts are being made to salvage them. More recently, Alan Bloom of Bressingham (England) has been working with the genus, producing some brilliant hybrids by crossing *C. masonorum*, *C.* 'Jackanapes', and *Curtonius paniculatus*, another gladioluslike South African plant. His red 'Lucifer' and 'Jenny Bloom' (gold with a red throat) are available in the United States. Of the older hybrids, I can find listed only 'Emily McKenzie', another yellow with red throat. Seed is to be had of *Crocosmia crocosmiiflora*.

Crocosmia 'Lucifer' is always said to be hardy through zone 5, but when I trustingly left my 'Lucifers' to sleep in the new garden over the winter they died to a man. I'm ordering more of them and the species *masonorum* (or *masoniorum*) for next year and will certainly dig them with the dahlias in the fall. I must add that a friend in a nearby town tells me that they overwinter outdoors for her, and that they're multiplying. Furthermore, Patrick Lima leaves his corms safely underground all winter in his garden on the Bruce Peninsula in Canada—but then, he has not only Lake Huron on three sides to temper the cold, but also has very sandy soil, and as we all know, drainage is one of the most important factors in the determination of hardiness.

I come now to another plant I formerly viewed with disapproval, perhaps as a result of having gazed for long periods of time at some of the less ingratiating members of the genus when, as a child, I sat swinging my legs on a park bench, waiting for my father to pick me up after art lessons. I remember only that cannas seemed to me to be too big, too bold, and much too sure of themselves. Perhaps they cowed me. I preferred daisies and violets and lily-of-the-valley. But cannas have come a long way since my early encounter with them. I can now regard them with an unprejudiced eye, although it still bothers me that their flowers, while certainly colorful, don't seem to have any particular plan in mind. They look as if they started out to be trumpets, then decided against it. But not everyone holds this lack of definition against them, obviously, for one sees them triumphantly emerging from their circular beds on front lawns all over the country, a real testimonial to the devotion of their owners when one considers that, in much of the land, they must be dug and

A *richly colored and textured canna with the name of 'Red King Humbert'.*

A *huge canna* (Canna warscewiczii) *presides over a group that contains* Ligularia tangutica *'The Rocket', annual rudbeckias, and* Lobelia *'Compliment Scarlet'.*

stored over the cold season, and many Americans still have a strong aversion to what they call "yard work." Clearly, these plants are admired and cherished, and not just by park planners. They are certainly imposing and just about as flamboyant as a plant can get.

There are many named hybrids of this tropical genus on the market. You can find two-foot to eight-foot cannas with flowers of yellow, orange, red, or bicolor. (You can even find them in pastel colors now, but that's not what we're looking for.) Their enormous leaves come in green, bronze, or several colors at once. I've found a one-hundred-dollar specimen whose fantastic variegations sound unbelievably bizarre—but there, we're straying from the path. Variegated leaves do not look appropriate in my hot garden, although I suppose it's possible they might in some-one else's.

If I had room, I'd try a two-foot canna, also called (like the crocosmia) 'Lucifer'. It has chrome-yellow petals with scarlet centers. Or 'Wisley Dwarf', with "curva-ceous" foliage and reddish orange blossoms. Is there room in the garden for them, possibly, or room in the cellar for more tubers?

In my garden I don't have tulips because they would be blooming almost alone. That doesn't mean that they can't be used in other hot-color gardens where their brilliant hues would start off the season's show with a bang.

The garden at Stonecrop is large enough to include cannas, purple berberis, red orach, and castor plant.

PLANT LIST: BULBS, CORMS, AND TUBERS

1   *Canna* 'Lucifer', 'Wisley Dwarf', and others
2   *Cosmos atrosanguineus*
3   *Crocosmia* 'Lucifer', *C. masonorum*, 'Emily McKenzie'
4   *Dahlia* 'Ellen Houston', 'Bishop of Llandaff', 'Japanese Bishop', 'Firebird', 'G. F. Hemerick', 'Venice', 'Crossfield Ebony', 'Envy', 'Rip City'
5   *Gladiolus* 'Robinetta', 'Comet', 'Amanda Mahy'
6   *Lilium pumilum (tenuifolium)*, *L. lancifolium (tigrinum)*, *L.* 'Elite', 'America', 'Grand Paradiso, 'Enchantment', 'Black Beauty'
7   *Oxalis triangularis* (see also chapter 8)
8   *Sprekelia formosissima*
9   tulips, fritillarias, tuberous begonias, caladiums (see also chapter 7)

7

A SEMISHADED GARDEN

So far, we've talked mostly about making a sunny garden of hot colors—but wouldn't it be possible to make one in the shade? The answer is yes, with qualifications. Such a garden cannot be as brilliant as one in full sun, since fewer bright-colored, temperate-climate plants grow in woodlands.

Shade gardens can be located either in the shade of a building or under trees. In the latter case the trees must have their lower branches removed, as very few ornamental plants will tolerate being closely loomed over by foliage of trees or shrubs. Woodland flowers shun the direct rays of the summer sun but do require *light*. There are only a few, such as European ginger, that actually enjoy dark, gloomy shade.

The trees in your woodland garden should be deciduous since most evergreens, besides casting too dense a shade, are surface-rooted. Furthermore, deciduous trees will allow the plants growing under them to have sunlight in the spring, when they want it, and protection from the sun in summer.

If you are planning to have a hot-color garden in shade provided by a building, you will have only to make sure the soil is suitable before drawing up your plans. But if it is to be under trees, more preparation will be necessary.

In the first place, don't even think about gardening under trees such as maple, locust, willow, catalpa, or any other tree that is a surface feeder unless you're content to grow nearly all of your plants in containers. Even trees that are not surface-rooted take up an awful lot of moisture, especially during the periods of high temperatures and very little rainfall. Woodland gardens have to be given extra waterings, even when gardens in full sun don't require it. If you were to make your garden under trees whose feeder roots were close to the surface, you'd have to water and fertilize constantly—and even then many of your plants would mope and might not survive.

But let us say you have a fine grove of trees that will give no more trouble than any trees are bound to give; perhaps they are oak, ash, hawthorn (*Crataegus viridis* is tall and spreading), or hackberry. They must be widely spaced and should be relieved of their lower branches. Underbrush must be removed and planting areas prepared by digging out superficial roots and rocks. Unless you find, miraculously, that the soil is already black, rich, and fluffy, you'll have to add and work in old manure, peat, topsoil, rotted leaves—whatever you can find to make it hospitable to your shade-loving plants, most of which need a moisture-retentive, humusy soil. When all this has been done, you can sit down and think about what you want to put where. Ideally, the whole garden will be carefully planned on paper—at least at the outset—paths charted and the plantings thought out, so that you will have the repetition of form and color that will hold the composition together. Sticking in plants with no consideration of harmonious combinations and repetition of theme will never produce a satisfying picture.

In chapter 8, on containers, we will discuss nonhardy plants that prefer filtered light or part shade: nasturtiums, columnea, tuberous begonias, oxalis, fuchsias, caladiums, and coleus. These subjects could very well be used here; common plants, such as nasturtiums, could be planted in the ground, while tuberous begonias, columneas, and fuchsias could be kept in pots or planters. In this semishaded garden we can happily use plants that don't look quite right in the sunny hot-color garden—astilbes and heucheras, for starters.

There are several deep red astilbes besides little 'Fanal': taller ones such as 'Spinell', 'Gertrude Brix', 'Glow' (a translation of the German *Glut*), 'Montgomery', 'Red Light', and 'Red Sentinel'. It's a good idea to get several different cultivars, as they don't all bloom at the same time. Be sure to give them your richest, fluffiest soil and mulch them well. They have shallow roots and need to be kept moist. I find that throwing a handful of organic fertilizer over them in early spring makes a big difference in their performance. Astilbes will look perfectly wretched by late July unless they are carefully tended and given lots of water.

You'll find quite a few brilliant red coralbells: *Heuchera* 'Pluie de Feu', mentioned previously, 'Mt. St. Helens', and one that's called 'Something Special', the brightest red of all. Heucheras have the endearing quality of blooming almost all summer if you'll take the time to remove their spent flower stems.

As in the sunny garden, we can cool and enrich our color combinations by adding purple-foliaged plants: the heucheras, hibiscus, and anthriscus mentioned in chapter 4. All of them enjoy a bit of shade.

I've had trouble keeping geums, but many other gardeners in this area do not. Orange *Geum x borisii* is the toughest one, I believe, but there are many other oranges and reds. You could try 'Fire Opal' or, better yet, eighteen-inch 'Red Wings', a semidouble scarlet that blooms longer than any of the others. If given rich, moist soil in semishade, it should flower from May to September. If you live in the warm side of zone 5, in zone 6, or farther south, you might allow yourself to be giddy and order a number of these to make a brave show.

This garden is the perfect place for *Lobelia cardinalis*, which you can grow in large colonies. If it is satisfied—that is, if it has light, rich, well-drained yet moist soil—it will self-sow. In any case you can harvest some seed every year to plant in flats, thus making sure of having new plants every spring. Another good method of insurance is to divide the clumps in April or May. Cardinal flowers make your task easy by multiplying their rosettes rather than simply making fatter clumps, as many perennials do. Instead of being obliged to attack them with a butcher knife and mallet, you can fork up the plants and gently wiggle apart the individual rosettes, each supplied with a set of stout, short, white roots, and replant them immediately. Nothing to it.

I mulch cardinal flowers with pine needles in autumn and try to keep them well watered at all times. In fact, there's scarcely anything I wouldn't do to please and preserve the gorgeous creatures. Set aglow by the slanting rays of the afternoon sun, their tall spikes of intricately designed blossoms, redder against the shadows of the woods garden than the churchmen's robes in a Raphael painting, are a sight that is ample reward for any trouble taken in their behalf.

There are many new cultivars of this American native, among which I have yet to find one that will survive the winter here. I'm tempted, just the same, to try a "garnet red" one called 'Ruby Slippers', said to bloom longer than the species, and also 'Royal Robe', which claims to be the only one with maroon foliage that is hardy in cold climates.

Another plant with blossoms of unmitigated red is *Spigelia marilandica*, a wildflower of the Southeast that, fortunately, is happy in the North as well. Since its lovely, open, trumpet-shaped, upward-facing, yellow-centered flowers are not *so* showy as those of cardinal flower, you will have to group several plants together to achieve the desired effect. They will bloom in June, to your delight.

*C*ardinal flowers enliven the edge of the woods garden.

If you plant several kinds of trollius near your spigelias, you'll be almost sure of having some of them blooming at the same time. Globeflowers probably do best in boggy soil in full sun but do not seem to mind living either in full sun or semishade under ordinary garden conditions, at least here in the North. They definitely do not like heat, so are not appropriate for gardens in the deep South. Even here, though they bloom well, I admit that in my border their handsome, palmate, toothed leaves look pretty tacky by the end of August. This probably wouldn't happen in the lightly shaded garden if they were planted in rich humus and were kept moist. Some trollius have petals (sepals, actually) that curve around, almost closing at the top to form a globe, while others open out flat, making a disk shape from which large, gold stamens spring up. Most of the nursery cultivars are hybrids derived from several species, although it is possible to find the pure species and their nonhybrid cultivars. I love the pale lemon-yellow *T. europaeus* in the border, but now we require *ledebourii* with orange-yellow flowers and lacy leaves that are cleft to the very stem. A three- to four-foot plant, usually listed as *T. l.* 'Golden Queen', carries splendid gleaming flowers, three to four inches across. Of the hybrids, *T. x cultorum*, you'd be well advised to get at least three or five each, if possible: early 'Etna' (two to five feet), 'Goldquelle' (a shorter one), and especially 'Orange Princess'. But some of the deepest orange flowers come on a German cultivar, 'Fireglobe' ('Feuertroll'). Then there's another vibrant orange one, 'Salamander'.

Trollius are the very devil to raise from seed, but once you have the plants you'll find them to be disease-free and long-lived.

For lowering the temperature, one dark purple perennial that enjoys part shade where summers are hot is monkshood (aconitum). There are many hybrids, species, and named cultivars of this genus to choose from, but since we'd like to have one that is a dark color and inclined to bloom around the same time as the cardinal flowers, I believe that *Aconitum x bicolor* 'Bressingham Spire' or 'Newry Blue' might be the answer. And why not try both? The first, one of Alan Bloom's creating, is a fine, compact three-footer whose hooded flowers of violet blue are produced over a very long period of time on stems that rarely require staking. 'Newry Blue' is a little darker and a little earlier to bloom but just as sturdy and upright as 'Bressingham Spire'. The leaves on this hybrid are particularly attractive, being dark, glossy, and deeply lobed.

You could, as well, plant monkshoods that bloom later and combine them with a swathe of *Salvia coccinea* 'Lady in Red', a plant that does just as well in light shade as in full sun.

Have you ever dealt with ligularias? I've decided it's really no use trying to grow them unless you have a spot they'll be happy in, and it's not easy to make a ligularia happy. Since they are uncommonly large, noble, imposing plants, their misery shows when they're miserable. The sight of their big leathery leaves drooping despondently is a sore trial to the gardener with a strong sense of parental responsibility.

These natives of China and Japan want deep, rich, very moist soil and are most content when growing on the edge of that often referred to (by garden writers) but seldom possessed (by gardeners) pond or stream. In regions where summers are hot, ligularias must be sited in semishade, and even then, and even when rain has been falling for days, the wretched things let go of their leaves as soon as the sun touches them, allowing them to hang down wearily like the ears of a sick elephant.

I have two ligularias—*L. japonica* and *L. stenocephala (przewalskii)* 'The Rocket'—which I've tried for a number of years, without success, to please. I even (after getting the idea from a garden magazine) built them big plastic bathtubs by digging great holes that I lined with heavy plastic before filling them in with an especially delicious soil mixture of loam, peat, and old cow manure. This act of loving care cheered them to a degree but not enough, I thought, to have made all that digging worthwhile. Nevertheless, the *L. japonica*, while often struggling with depression, does unfailingly decorate itself every summer with the most astonishing, wide-awake, orange-yellow daisies, three to three and a half inches across. This species is a four- to five-foot sterile plant with cordate leaves, twice lobed and serrated. The daisies appear on loose panicles in June, earlier than those of any other ligularia.

Although 'The Rocket', a cultivar of *Ligularia stenocephala (przewalskii)*, is a splendid plant, with its tall, black stalks packed with small, yellow blossoms, we won't consider it here since its flowers are too citron for this color scheme.

If you are already acquainted with this genus, you know that there are species with cultivars that are handsomer than mine. *L. dentata* 'Othello' and 'Desdemona' both form basal rosettes of one-foot, leathery, kidney-shaped, sharply toothed leaves on one-foot purple stalks. The leaves are also purple in spring but retain that color only on their undersides through the summer. Both cultivars have larger (four-inch), deeper orange daisies than the species I have, and they are also more compact.

'Othello', at three feet, is smaller than 'Desdemona', which can attain four. (What a mystery are the mental processes of those who name plants!) There are lots of other small ligularia species and cultivars such as *Ligularia dentata* 'Orange Queen' with green foliage and *L.* 'Gregynog Gold', which can reach six feet and carries its bright orange flowers on upright, conical inflorescences. The cordate leaves are elegantly veined.

Are you good at growing pansies? I can't brag about my own record in this department, but I long to learn the trick. I've always blamed the hot weather when mine have pined away, even though I've been told that other gardeners with the same weather succeed. I had decided I could very well live without pansies, until I saw some celestial blue ones in shallow, gray stone bowls perched on low pillars at Dumbarton Oaks—so beautiful, I wanted to carry them home.

Breeders have been making great strides in their efforts to make pansies not only larger, brighter, and longer blooming, but more heat-tolerant as well. There may be some hope for me. Still, this semishaded garden would give them the best chance of living a healthy life in areas with a continental climate where they must cope with extremes of temperature. One could plant them directly in the ground or in containers. They come in such astonishing colors nowadays—our mothers wouldn't recognize them. Luckily for us, many of the new strains or cultivars are unashamedly orange, incandescent red, warm yellow, or "black." One called *Viola* 'Padparadja' is as exotic as its name in a color that the seed company that developed it can only describe as "gripping"; which is not the adjective my daughter would have used. She grew them last summer and had me get down close to them so I could enjoy their sweet scent as well as their brilliant color. 'Spanish Sun' looks, in the photograph, as if it might set the page on fire. 'Brunig' has petals of burnt red, edged with gold, while a velvety black one has a bright yellow eye. The most dramatic of all is one named 'Jolly Joker', a really droll little thing whose lower petals are a vivid, dark tangerine, while the upper ones are deep purple.

Impatiens, too, have undergone many changes of character since their princi-pally pastel days. There is at least one clear orange called 'Tango', a lovely plant that I've seen combined with *Ipomoea batatas* 'Blackie' at Cornell Plantations, where the container plantings are so wonderfully designed by Dianne Miske. There is a new impatiens, 'Mega Orange Star', that I would *not* use; the white star is too strongly defined and would, I think, be distracting. You can browse through your local gar-den centers and greenhouses for impatiens in the colors you need, or look in Stokes's and Park's catalogs for seed of separate colors: red, scarlet, and orange. I found a scarlet one that I put in small, hanging containers on the shaded side of the fence and also in pots. It's a good red whose name, I regret to say, is 'Blitz 2000'.

The 'Shady Lady' series will carry masses of two-inch flowers, even when planted in deep shade. Those called 'Pride' have even larger flowers, bloom earlier, and go on blooming and remaining compact until very late in the season. This type wants medium to light shade.

The New Guinea impatiens will take more sun than the others and in fact bloom better with some sun, but even they prefer filtered light. Some of them have

Impatiens *'Tango' with* Ipomoea batatas *'Blackie'.*

variegated leaves that might detract from the color of the flowers and foliage we are working with, so consider very carefully before you buy seeds or plants. There are some new hybrids with less brilliantly variegated foliage—'Tango' is one of these and has deep green leaves with purplish undertones.

I couldn't very well use tulips in my sunny garden since it doesn't get going soon enough, but they would be fine additions to this garden, starting with species tulips such as red *Tulipa linifolia* and *T. praestans* 'Fusilier'. There are early, midseason, and late tulips in red, deep yellow, and a black-purple that will, if your springs are cool, carry on for several weeks. Here where we often get spells of 80 and 90 degrees Fahrenheit in May, neither tulips nor primulas have a chance to do their best. Not that that stops us from growing them.

If you plant your yellow tulips in the midst of a colony of the native columbine, *Aquilegia canadensis*, you'll find that, combined with clouds of those delicate, red-and-yellow blossoms, they make a fine tapestry effect. Be sure you don't plant any other columbine nearby, or they will all recklessly interbreed. I installed McKana Hybrids not far away from my *A. canadensis*, with the result that I now have masses of wonderfully and variously colored tall columbines, but no longer do I have *canadensis*, pure and unsullied.

Speaking of primulas—avoid the reds by all means, unless you are able to get hold of the very dark velvety red that is found in the 'Cowichan' strain of polyanthas. The reds, at least all I've seen in the *Primula vulgaris* and ordinary *polyantha* strains, are of an unsuitable rosy hue. *P. elatior* or oxlip, however, does hang bright red and yellow blossoms from its tall stems. Strong, yellow *polyanthas* are easy to find.

But back to bulbs. What about fritillarias, those astonishing-looking ones that grow three feet tall and are called *Fritillaria imperialis* or crown imperials? Each stem carries, on top, like a crown, a circle or umbel of large, down-hanging, red, yellow, or orange bells with tapered petals, from which protrude the stigma. On the very top of the inflorescence rises a cluster of slender, erect leaves resembling, in effect,

The native columbine, Aquilegia canadensis, *will self-sow among tulips in a lightly shaded woodland area.*

the crest of a hoopoe bird. "Spectacular" is the word usually applied to these plants and, in this case, is appropriate. *F. i.* 'Rubra Maxima' (red) and 'The Premier' (burnt orange) or 'Aurora' would be the best ones to use here.

Crown imperials are somewhat tender and would have to be thickly mulched in zone 5. Another problem is that they like sun; however, I should think that, grown under trees such as oak that are slow to leaf out in spring, they'd get enough sun to satisfy them. They go dormant in midsummer, which means they don't have to have many months of sunlight. It also means you'll have to plan for some sturdy late bloomers to surround them and hide the sight of their withering foliage.

This summer I grew *Nierembergia* 'Purple Robe' from seed, thinking to provide carpets of small, purple flowers for lightly shaded areas of the garden. I set some of the plants in the ground, and some I put in pots. By mid-August I had, perhaps, on my ten or so plants about six blossoms in all, most of them *lavender*, what's more. A fizzle. I was wailing about this failure in plant performance to a visitor who happens to run a garden center. She said she gets white nierembergias from growers, pots and grows them on, and soon has luxuriantly blooming potted plants for her customers. On hearing this, I stopped berating the seed company and set to wondering what I had done wrong. I hope to find someone who will be able to tell me the secret of making nierembergias look like the pictures in the catalogs. Of course, I'll try again only if I can find seed that will produce real purple flowers.

Many years ago I sent for seedling Exbury azaleas from that excellent seed, shrub, and tree nursery, Girard's of Ohio. (I used to get all kinds of "baby" shrubs from them at, if I remember correctly, three for a dollar and a quarter—and they're not much more now—shrubs that are today providing beauty and structure to my garden.) These small azaleas were cheap because, having been grown from seed rather than cuttings, their color and blossom size would be unpredictable. My azaleas all turned out to be brilliant oranges and deep yellows, gorgeous indeed but inappropriate, since my whole garden was pastel at the time. I gave them away. Now I'm thinking how perfect they'd be for our present project. I'm looking apprecia- tively at pictures of azaleas called 'Fireflash', 'Vulcan's Flame', 'Hot Shot'. As you shop for azaleas, make sure you get the correct information as to their resistance to cold. I've found the deciduous sorts to be happier here than the evergreens.

Another wonderful shrub for this garden is kalmia. Our native *Kalmia latifolia*, or mountain laurel, comes in shades of pink and white, but breeders have, in the last few years, made some big changes. When one looks at the new offerings, one is dazzled by their colors and patterns but soon sees that the strong color is mostly in the flower buds, which open to pink or white blossoms. One, at least, 'Kaleido- scope', has red buds that open red; several of them would be mighty impressive.

PLANT LIST: A SEMISHADED GARDEN

1 *Aconitum x bicolor* 'Bressingham Spire', 'Newry Blue'
2 *Aquilegia canadensis*
3 *Astilbe* 'Fanal', 'Spinell', 'Glow', 'Red Light', 'Red Sentinel'
4 *Azalea* 'Fireflash', 'Vulcan's Flame', and others
5 *Fritillaria imperialis* 'Rubra Maxima', 'The Premier', 'Aurora'
6 *Geum x borisii*, G. 'Fire Opal', 'Red Wings'
7 *Heuchera* 'Pluie de Feu', 'Mt. St. Helens', 'Something Special' (and purple-foliaged varieties)
8 *Impatiens* 'Tango', 'Blitz 2000', 'Shady Lady', and 'Pride' strains
9 *Kalmia latifolia* 'Kaleidoscope'
10 *Ligularia japonica*, *L. stenocephala*, *L. dentata* 'Desdemona', 'Othello', 'Orange Queen', *L.* 'Gregynog Gold'
11 *Lobelia cardinalis* and cultivars
12 *Primula polyantha*, *P. p.* 'Cowichan', *P. elatior*
13 *Spigelia marilandica*
14 *Trollius ledebourii*, *T. l.* 'Golden Queen', *T. x cultorum* 'Etna', 'Goldquelle', Orange Princess', 'Fireglobe', 'Salamander'
15 *Tropaeolum* 'Empress of India', 'Whirlybird' strain
16 *Tulipa linifolia*, *T. praestans* 'Fusilier', and others
17 *Viola* 'Padparadja', 'Jolly Joker', 'Spanish Sun', 'Brunig'
18 fuchsia, caladium, tuberous begonia, coleus, *Oxalis triangularis*

8

CONTAINERS

I f you are thinking seriously of making an enclosed hot-color garden, you'll want to cram it as full as possible with brilliant color. The aim of this garden is to produce the opposite effect to that of, say, Stourhead and Luten Hoo, in England, or any of the other great park gardens of Capability Brown and his school. We are not now attempting to clear away distractions, to open up wide, cool vistas, or to engender a feeling of peace and serenity, but quite the contrary. The key word here is "impact." Our purpose is to stimulate, to shock, rather than to soothe. The effect of the garden will be therapeutic, certainly, and although it is strong medicine, it will be taken in small doses. For this, then, you'll want to fill all of the available space, both horizontal and vertical, with plants that will contribute generously to the three-dimensional picture you are creating. The use of plants in containers as well as in the ground will be a great help in carrying out this project.

In considering which plants to use, let us begin by looking at those that are most often grown in pots. First to mind come geraniums (pelargoniums), surely the gayest and most obliging plants in the world. And they do duty all over the world, tumbling from pots and window boxes throughout the Americas, Europe, Africa, and the Middle East, at least. I used to trim back the geranium bushes in Algiers and throw the cuttings down a shaggy slope, where they simply rolled over, rooted themselves, and went on blithely blooming, summer and winter. In Switzerland geraniums foam out of window boxes, even on barns, office buildings, and department stores, to say nothing of huge planters on the streets. In Italy you will see them on staircases, balconies, and in pots held by iron rings that are set into the outside walls of grim old stone buildings whose aspect they do much to lighten. In Turkey our landlord, who adored flowers, had to do all his gardening in containers since the walled court around our three-story apartment house was paved. He had pots, boxes, and large recycled olive oil tins sitting all over the court (even on the chicken house) and on every outside stair, all the way up to the third floor. They overflowed with flowers: agapanthus, jasmine, lantana, but principally geraniums of every color and shape.

And now in this country, in all those pretty towns that have been tidied up, refurbished, and repainted (in "Williamsburg" colors), window boxes and half barrels have been installed along Main Street, while containers have been hung from decorative iron lampposts, all filled, almost inevitably, except for a few petunias and dusty millers, with geraniums. Was there ever such a handy plant?

You can find ivy-leaved and ordinary geraniums in many shades of vibrant red and even orange ('Orangesonne' and 'Prince of Orange'), as well as in a deep velvety red that is almost black ('Royal Blood' and 'Black Lace'), the flowers of the latter having orange stamens. Some of these pelargoniums have the bonus of dark red foliage. I take cuttings of mine in late summer but also cut back and root-prune large plants in autumn, then repot them to winter over indoors. They make enormous bushes in the garden the following summer.

Years ago in Maryland in my first attempt at a flower garden, I planted petunias, pink ones and white, that I'd bought in flats at a garden shop. I was so impressed by their ebullient, unflagging outpouring of color and fragrance that ever since I've felt indebted to them for helping to impel me toward gardening as a vocation. The sense of obligation continued even after I thought myself to have left petunias far behind—and beneath—me as I soared upward to associate with more esoteric genera.

(The fact is that one is hardly to be blamed for snobbery in this case, since gas station and toll booth planters have every year been displaying bigger, fatter, and ever more doubled, dandified, and distorted specimens to the point where it's no wonder we've been put off petunias.) Then a summer or two ago all the discriminating gardeners started to grow the charming little plum-pink species, *Petunia integrifolia,* which caused a lot of us to reconsider the genus. So when I came upon a plain purple petunia ('Primetime Blue') of normal size and shape disporting itself among the perennials in the red-and-purple garden at Stonecrop, I was ready to applaud rather than to

Petunia *'Primetime Blue' will pick up and repeat the color of clematis you may have in your garden.*

hoot. What a great idea! And how well they would do in my planters. Later, when I discovered a flat of 'Midnight Dreams' at our garden store, I snapped them up immediately.

There are many red petunias that will *not* do, having too much blue in their makeup, but one called 'Ultra Red' is purer and would harmonize very well with the other plants. There are probably other pure reds whose names I don't know. As for purples, only the darkest will suit. There's one, 'Plum Carpet', in a "floribunda" series designated 'Celebrity' that looks to be just the thing, but you'll doubtless find others swarming out of six-packs at your local garden center next spring.

Petunias are lovable not only for their prettiness and their fragrance but because, while appearing to be delicate—almost fragile—they are extremely tough, nearly invincible, never giving up, never lowering the flag no matter what hits them—wind and rain, one-hundred-degree heat and 97 percent humidity. A commendable attitude, you'll have to admit.

It's decidedly not a new idea to use verbenas in containers, but it was new to me last summer when I decided they might make good additions to the uninhibited color scheme. I knew that they wanted full sun, and that they don't in the least object to high temperatures, that they adapt themselves easily to living in pots, and that they bloom nonstop all summer long. I knew also that while many verbenas are winter-hardy in the South, here one would have to bring them indoors for the cold months or take cuttings—preferably the latter—if one wanted to hang on to them.

I looked them up, and found that Clausen/Ekstrom say: "This predominantly tropical or semi-tropical genus is best known for its gaudy hybrids, so frequently grown as bedding plants" (p. 559). Sounded as though we were made for each other. I took the plunge and ordered some red ones and 'Homestead Purple'.

Now I think I *do* have a legitimate complaint against people who sell verbena 'Homestead Purple'—or perhaps my complaint should be against the person who gave it its name. I bought several plants, put them in the new garden, and had to

V erbena 'Romance Scarlet' is royally accommodated in a shallow Italian rolled-rim pot. Zinnia 'Old Mexico' to the left, Tagetes 'Favourite' to the right.

transfer them to the front of the long border when they began to burst out in *lavender*. The red that I bought, 'Romance Scarlet', was a great success, however, filling huge pots with abundant flaming flowers, on and on.

The opposite, toothed, hairy leaves of most verbenas account for much of their appeal. Montrose Nursery used to offer many species and cultivars of verbena, the descriptions of which almost made one want to move south. I tried a red one, *Verbena peruviana*, that the nursery thought would be hardy through zone 5, putting it on a wall that it glorified beautifully for a summer, but where it failed to reappear the following spring.

But why limit oneself to plants offered by nurseries? How about growing verbenas from seed? There are seeds for scarlets and purples (maybe real purple), although germinating them sounds a bit tricky. They need to be kept in the dark in warm soil (seventy degrees Fahrenheit) for twenty days, which wouldn't be easy in my house— but then, think of all the practically free plants one would have if one made it work.

As you search the seed catalogs you'll find various "series" of verbena seeds— 'Romance', 'Imagination', 'Amour', and others—so you'll be hard put to it to choose. The red in the series called 'Novalis' looks the best, at least the brightest, to me. If I were you, I'd get the scarlet without the white eye; the white looks pretty insistent in the photograph.

Another ordinary plant you could include in your pots or baskets is one that is grown only for its purple foliage, *Secreasea pallida* or 'Purple Heart', mentioned in chapter 4, a sprawling subject with long, slender, pointed leaves that sheath its jointed stems. It looks like tradescantia, or simply a large form of wandering Jew, and is a most cooperative plant: put pieces of it in a jar of water, and they will forthwith send out roots; cut it off below a joint, press the cut section into the earth, and it will promptly start to grow. Cascading from a container on the garden fence (along with something red or orange), it would pick up and echo the foliage color of perilla, dahlias, and opal basil that will be growing in beds below.

Speaking of purple foliage, don't forget the oxalis (*Oxalis triangularis*), mentioned in chapter 4. You can plant the corms, several to a pot, to set next to small plants with flame-colored blossoms, preferably in light shade.

And if you have cool, semishaded spots in your garden, or areas that receive filtered or only morning sunlight, you'll be able to use nasturtiums (tropaeolum), most of which come in just the right colors. There are many types, some trailing, some climbing, some bushy. A particularly jewel-like variety is 'Empress of India', whose flowers are dark, velvety crimson, or orange-yellow. 'Whirlybird' mixes come in orange, gold, and scarlet. For our present purpose we should, I think, avoid the pas-

Nasturtiums seem to want sun in the spring and filtered light only during periods of intense heat, so it's handy to grow them in movable pots.

*C*lematis vie for space on the fence at the far end of the garden. Beneath them nasturtiums enjoy *protection from the sun.*

tel strains. Be sure, when planting nasturtiums, not to make the soil too rich, which promotes the production of leaves rather than flowers. The climbing sorts could be grown up a trellis if you like, instead of trailing out of pots or hanging baskets.

By the way, have you seen the fine black netting that can be tacked to a fence or supported by posts? It can be used instead of trellises and works very well for clematis, so should serve, as well, for nasturtiums.

Before ending this discussion of ordinary plants, I should add that chrysanthemums, calendulas, zinnias, and marigolds can be—and often are—used in containers. If you choose cultivars that are short and bushy, you'll be better pleased with the results. I, for one, am firmly opposed to the use of tall, leggy plants in containers that raise them above ground level.

I mentioned earlier that I plan to use the miniature dahlias as container plants next summer, but they are not the only tubers that can be handled this way. Tuberous begonias thrive in pots too. Like nasturtiums, they like dappled light and dislike heat. Their soil should be fluffy and peaty and should not be allowed to dry out. I used to grow these plants in a window box in semishade where they were cooler than they would be in the new garden, where I daren't put them. They do come in red, orange, and yellow. If you'll resist buying the huge, fringed, ruffled ones and can try to track down smaller specimens with simpler shapes, you'll find them to be more in the spirit of this garden. The others look to me as if they should be topping off ornate urns at Versailles. Boucher would have liked to paint them.

If you've never grown coleus, this might be a good time to experiment with it. It does come in wild and wonderful colors now. You could either grow it from seed (Stokes offers seed for separate color combinations rather than confining you to mixes), or you might prefer to search for suitable specimens in garden centers. It goes without saying that you can plant coleus in the flower bed if you prefer, but since it spends most of its life in the North in pots, it seemed natural to include it in this chapter. It's so content in pots—doesn't seem always to be yearning for freedom as some plants do when confined. Content it is, I must add, if the pots are in semishade.

It's easy to find coleus in the right colors.

I've always admired caladiums, those tropical American plants that are grown for their large, variously colored, heart-shaped leaves. I admired but did not covet them. For while I thought they looked perfectly marvelous in my brother's court-yard in New Orleans, I felt them to be inappropriate to a New York farmhouse parlor and garden. But it now occurs to me that red-leaved caladiums would be very effective in the filtered light of the kind of garden we're planning. There are probably half a hundred hybrid caladiums to choose from, but the best for our purposes appears to be eighteen-inch 'Frieda Hemple', whose crimson leaves are edged with green. The tubers from which these plants grow can be planted and left in the ground in the South, but in the North they must be lifted and overwintered, like dahlia tubers, in a cool basement. Alternatively, they can be kept in pots in the parlor, to set out when the weather turns warm in spring. They make nice house-plants for those who have a sunny, warm place large enough to accommodate them.

The use of containers, on the ground or on the wall or fence, will enable you to include more plants, obviously, and help you to keep the color coming as the peren-nials bow out. You will, moreover, be able to shift plants such as nasturtiums from the shady spots they want during the hottest part of the summer to the full sun that will, in fall, be good for them and will promote a final burst of bloom.

Using plants in containers will have the added advantage of giving you a chance to try some exotic stuff from Logee's or other mail-order vendors of tropical won-ders—to say nothing of your local greenhouse. Of course, unless you live in the South, you can't go overboard on tender plants unless you have a greenhouse your-self, or plant lights or a bay window—or you don't mind buying new plants every year.

If you are a southerner, you are no doubt familiar with many plants that would be easily adapted to our purpose and will have no trouble wintering them over. Most of us northerners, however, will have to do some research and contrive ways of keep-ing our imported acquisitions happy during long months of cold temperatures and gray skies. As we search through greenhouses and plant lists for suitable subjects, we must be sure to select those that will bloom during the months when their color will be needed in our gardens; a plant that's going to bloom gloriously under lights all winter and spend the summer in the garden quietly recuperating from its efforts is of no use at all for this project. I've been doing a little research myself since I intend to branch out next year, to graduate, tentatively, from my cherished geraniums. Not that I intend to jettison the geraniums, which have been cascading from containers all over the garden, unfailingly, unstintingly supplying masses of color, all through spring, summer, and fall. Next summer I'll jam them into odd corners when and where needed, but I intend to fill some of my fanciest pots with more esoteric stuff, only hoping that I may succeed with it and that I won't have to go back to the geraniums muttering apologies, as I restore them to their former positions of eminence.

I want to try, for example, columneas, although I realize I'll have to place them in semishaded spots as they object to excessive heat. Columnea foliage is most attractive, consisting of "chains" of small, pointed, opposite leaves, while its two-lipped blossoms come in shades of red and/or yellow. *Columnea* 'Bonfire' has shiny leaves and orange-and-yellow flowers. 'Campfire', an everblooming, red-flowered individual, has mahogany foliage, but the hybrid 'Evlo' has stems sporting "plush velvety leaves that swoop down and burst into quantities of flamboyant flaming red blossoms," according to the catalog. If only it does this in July and August. *C. arguta*'s flowers are also a brilliant red. Then there's *C. gloriosa* 'Superba'—goodness! How to choose? I'll try several, after ascertaining their blooming periods.

There's a new and improved version of Brazilian tibouchina, *Tibouchina urvilleana* 'Edwardsii', which promises compact form as well as wonderful furry, ribbed, gray leaves and an abundant supply of three-inch, flaring, five-petaled, royal purple flowers. This one is said to bloom all year round, but since the species blooms in summer, I imagine that's when this cultivar will be most enthusiastic. Besides, when I first encountered tibouchina, it was on a summer day when it was blooming beautifully in large pots outside the New York Botanical Garden.

I've got my eye on two scutellarias, one with orange-scarlet, yellow-throated flowers, the other with purple ones. Scutellaria, or skullcap, is a member of the mint family whose species are found growing pretty much all over the world. Some of the temperate zone species are garden worthy, while many are weedy, or at any rate modest plants whose hooded, usually lavender-blue flowers have a certain charm, perhaps, but don't really blow anyone away. Some of the tropical species, on the other hand, let out all the stops. The catalog writer who describes the orange-and-yellow *Scutellaria costaricana* fairly gibbers in his attempts to present its merits. The accompanying photograph certainly does justify him in his enthusiasm. The plant is said to be everblooming, so my only concern is lest it be too tall (two to three feet) to look good in a container.

The purple-flowering species *S. formosana (javanica)* is a smaller plant and no doubt is less flashy. It blooms not all year round but during the summer months.

How do you feel about miniature roses? I've never raised them, but they must have a large following, for new ones are constantly being invented. They do very well as pot plants, not objecting to confinement and blooming all summer as if they were annuals—at least, so I am told. If I were to get some for the new garden, I'd order one with petals that are orange on the top and yellow beneath, 'Pride and Joy'. Two other good strong yellows are 'Sun Splash' and 'Charm Bracelet'. 'Starina', a Meilland creation, is scarlet. Roses, whether large or small, are not painless, you must remember; they are loved not only by people but by bugs, including Japanese beetles, and by the smaller creatures that produce mildew, black spot, and many other plant afflictions. Miniature roses fare better in this respect than hybrid teas, but not better than shrub roses, which are not exactly pest-free.

If you can find some orange thunbergia (*Thunbergia alata aurantiaca*) at your local greenhouse or garden center, you can use them either in hanging baskets or in pots, in full sun or light shade. Since they are really vines, they should be placed high enough so that they can spill out of their containers and trail down. In the North we grow thunbergias as annuals, but they are perennial vines in the South, where they clamber over porches and trellises. Their simple, clean flowers with the dark central spot look so ingenuous—don't you agree? I'd like to have lots of them. Everywhere.

Fuchsias, on the other hand, have a sophisticated, a complicated look. I know that they are garden plants like any other in the South, and that there are hedges of them in Ireland—and one supposes elsewhere as well—but to me they remain somewhat strange. Or at least they did until this summer, when I came upon the upright *Fuchsia triphylla* 'Gartenmeister Bonstedt' in a local greenhouse. It was a young plant, not yet blooming, but I bought it for its beautiful foliage, not even knowing that it would soon add dangling umbels of what the *RHS Dictionary* calls cinnabar-red—slender, slightly flaring tubes that terminate in clusters of spiky petals. Since the stems and the undersides of the dark green, oblanceolate leaves are chianti purple, the total effect is most sumptuous—almost regal. Makes me think of those embroidered, slash-sleeved medieval tunics.

The fuchsia named 'Voodoo', in purple and crimson, would decorate a spot with filtered light, as would *F. magellanica ricartonii,* with flowers of the same colors. A small trailing one from New Zealand, *F. procumbens,* carries many purple blossoms rimmed with orange. 'Baby Chang' is a compact dwarf with orange bells, while 'Honeysuckle' has maroon leaves that dramatize its dangling, orange-red blossoms. Upright 'Swanley Yellow', a vigorous cultivar, carries brilliant vermilion-orange flowers. Do you have room in partly shaded areas for a few of them? If you prowl around nearby nurseries, you're sure to find a few fuchsias with blossoms of appropriate colors; or if not, you can send away for them.

Gardeners who live in mild regions, or those with greenhouses, could use abutilon hybrids. Northerners can keep them in large containers, moving them outdoors each spring. These relatives of hibiscus and hollyhocks produce their large, cup-shaped flowers on tender shrubs with maple-shaped leaves and have for many years been popular houseplants.

*S*plendid **Fuchsia triphylla** *'Gartenmeister Bonstedt Improved' lolls over* **Helichrysum italicum ssp. serotinum.**

Persian shield, which is a shrub in warm regions, makes an impressive greenhouse plant in the North and could be set out to help glorify a hot-color garden in the summer. This native of Burma has remarkable eight-inch-long, opposite leaves that are iridescent silver, crimson, and violet above, maroon on the undersides. Some forms of this plant (whose proper name is *Strobilanthes dyeranus*) are too pastel for this particular purpose, but others come in tones deep enough to harmonize with the rest of the garden.

Last spring a friend gave me two little rooted cuttings of a cuphea that we believe to be *C. ignea.* I put one in a pot and one in the ground, and by the end of the summer they were fine two-foot bushes, their many slender stems wonderfully ornamented with shiny slender tubular vermilion flowers that emerged in the axils of the slim, pointed, opposite leaves. Because the stems and leaves have dark red undertones, the whole effect is richly harmonious, at the same time having a festive look. Makes you think of firecrackers or of a Christmas tree with red candles. The outfacing flowers have a small, white ruffle inside their mouths, from which red stamens protrude.

But it's time to discuss, at least briefly, the containers that our plants are going to live in. In choosing them, rule number one should be to avoid anything that will pull the eye of the beholder away from the combinations of flower and foliage we've been so carefully orchestrating. A brown pot with bold designs in white, yellow, or blue, for example, would be dreadfully distracting. In the category of bad choices, I would place, in addition to containers decorated with colored patterns, those shaped like birds, animals, and, heaven help us, human heads. I would not use containers with a metallic sheen or those ribbed and fluted bowls, usually white, that perch on pinched-in, fluted stands. Nor would I hang receptacles of whatever material from silken, braided, woven, tufted, brightly hued cords—you know the kind—with a big long tassel at the bottom. Pots or boxes painted or glazed in solid colors must be chosen with extreme care lest they throw off the color scheme. While this garden aims for impact, it is definitely *not* a case of anything goes. If we want to give full value to flamboyant colors and color combinations, we must meticulously monitor their surroundings and not introduce any clamorously clashing or unrelated elements. Let the accessories be simple, muted, restrained, and leave it to the plants to put on the performance.

Terra-cotta pots are fine; Italian pots decorated with terra-cotta designs in high relief—lion's heads, garlands, etc., are fine since they embellish rather than detract from the plants they contain.

Until quite recently it has been hard to find attractive clay pots, here in the East, at any rate. Now, however, there is at least one company that is importing wonderful clay containers in every shape and size, including the long, rectangular ones with either simple or ornate designs. I like especially the "rolled-rim" pots from Italy, with either one roll or more. They are extraordinarily handsome—but then, there are many styles to choose from. These containers are similar if not identical to the very expensive pots and containers imported from Italy by some large nurseries. This New York company sells only wholesale; but you could no doubt talk the proprietor of your local garden center into ordering some of their wares.

One highly esteemed plant nursery I know sells large, blue-gray pots, plain or fancy, made of fiberglass, which sounds awful but looks quite inoffensive, even attractive. They have the advantage of enduring all weather changes without shattering (unlike clay pots, which northerners must store under cover during the winter) and of being lighter to handle than clay. Besides, since they're not porous, the plants they contain don't have to be watered so frequently. They are, however, expensive.

Plastic pots and planters have the same three advantages as the fiberglass ones but are never, to my mind, acceptable in a garden. One can, though, put a plastic pot down inside a clay one, to save work and at the same time preserve appearances. Some gardeners claim that because clay "breathes," plants grow better in clay pots than in plastic, but I've never been able to see any difference. I do know that some plants, such as watercress, like to have cool roots. Plastic pots get hot, especially dark ones, so are not suitable for such plants.

I've been looking for unobtrusive and lightweight containers to hang on or fasten to the fence and have turned up a few that look promising. There's a twenty-four-inch wire rectangular gadget, made to hold several pots in a row, there are light wooden wall planters, also rectangular. There are plenty of semicircular wire baskets meant to hold moss and plants that can live in it, as well as crescent-shaped, cup-shaped, and shell-shaped clay planters made to be attached to a wall or fence. I don't want to overdo this container business; too many small things hanging over or attached to the fence would make the garden look cluttered, or like a garden center gift shop. Perhaps I'll install two long, simple, window-box-type planters inside the garden on the east and west walls, then two outside, on either side of the gate where they'll be in part shade. Plants will trail down from these containers inside, while clematis, planted in the ground, will climb up beside them. That's the plan, anyway. These things don't always work out.

PLANT LIST: CONTAINERS

1　Abutilon hybrids
2　*Begonia tuberosa*
3　*Caladium* 'Frieda Hemple'
4　*Coleus*, various
5　*Columnea* 'Campfire', 'Bonfire', 'Evlo', *C. arguta*, *C. gloriosa* 'Superba'
6　*Cuphea ignea*
7　dahlia (miniature)
8　*Fuchsia triphylla* 'Gartenmeister Bonstedt', *F.* 'Voodoo', *F. magellanica ricartonii*, *F.* 'Baby Chang', *F. procumbens*, and others
9　*Oxalis triangularis*
10　*Pelargonium* (geranium), various
11　*Petunia* 'Midnight Dreams', 'Primetime Blue', and others
12　*Rosa* 'Pride and Joy', 'Sun Splash', 'Charm Bracelet', 'Starina' (all miniature)
13　*Scutellaria costaricana*, *S. formosana (javanica)*
14　*Setcreasea pallida* 'Purple Heart'
15　*Strobilanthes dyeranus*
16　*Thunbergia alata aurantiaca*
17　*Tibouchina urvilleana* 'Edwardsii'
18　*Tropaeolum* 'Empress of India' and 'Whirlybird'
19　*Verbena* 'Romance', 'Imagination', and others, in scarlet and purple

EPILOGUE— OCTOBER 14

It occurs to me as I contemplate the garden that it looks very much like an aging glamour girl, or—to use an expression of Horace Walpole's when describing Lady Mary Wortley in her later years—a dilapidated beauty. The garden is splendid still, in some ways: The dahlias are loaded with blossoms that glow like jewels, ruby and flame petals and garnet buds against wine-dark leaves. Spears of gladioli are still sending out fresh, fiery flowers and gomphrena is going full speed ahead as if it had had no intimations of an imminent demise, although the nights are chilly, and we've already had one frost. Chrysanthemums are still full of energy, and the marigolds are making a great conflagration along the walkways. Tempering all this riotous display, blue salvias continue to send up their serene violet spikes.

So why "dilapidated"? you may ask. Ah, well—the tithonias, for one thing, and tithonias are quite a presence, as I have said. By now their drooping, browning leaves and their ugly knobs of spent flowers (too numerous to remove unless one were to make it a full-time job) are a distressing sight. The heleniums, while showing a flicker of red or yellow here and there, are, without quite admitting it, finished for this year. The glow of *Heliopsis* 'Summer Sun' is also being extinguished, while the only daylily that struggles on is little 'Stella d'Oro', which, though game, looks pretty well beaten. Gaillardias haven't quite given up, nor has *Potentilla* 'Gold Star'.

The thing to do, I believe, is to perform a serious clean-up job out here. Come out with the wheelbarrow and pruning shears and bravely fell the tithonias, as if blind to the fact that they are still carrying many blossoms. Chop the heleniums and clear away the wilted daylily foliage. Then settle back on the bench to rejoice in the golden autumn sunlight, safe from the cold wind, within these walls, able for a little while longer to take satisfaction in the unblighted aspect of this secret jungle.

GARDEN
ACKNOWLEDGMENTS

All photographs were taken at Elisabeth Sheldon's garden except the following:

Colonial Williamsburg, Williamsburg, Va., p. 129; Cornell Plantations, Ithaca, N.Y., pp. 30, 35, 127, 138, plant combination design by Diane Miske, p. 73; Nancy Goodwin, Montrose Garden, Hillsborough, N.C., pp. 44, 71; Longwood Gardens, Kennett Square, Pa., pp. 33, 37, 42, 76, 96, 100, 109, 145; Jane Lumley Garden, Ithaca, N.Y., design by Barbara Martin, pp. 16, 74, 108; The New York Botanical Garden, Bronx, N.Y., pp. 32, 36 (bottom), 53, 60, 98, 99 (top), 99 (bottom), 112, 115, perennial border design by Lynden Miller, p. 113, plant combination design by Elizabeth Innvar, p. 27 (bottom); private garden, Southampton, N.Y., designers/gardeners Michael Doherty and Tish Rehill, Principals of Gardeneering, Inc., p. 61; Stonecrop Gardens, Cold Spring, N.Y., design by Caroline Burgess, pp. 116, 117, 135; Wave Hill, Bronx, N.Y., design by Marco Polo Stufano, p. 36 (top).

SOURCES FOR SEEDS, PLANTS, AND CONTAINERS

Forestfarm, 990 Tetherow Road, Williams, OR 97544

Girard Nurseries, P.O. Box 428, Geneva, OH 44041

J. L. Hudson, Seedsman, P.O. Box 1058, Redwood City, CA 94064

Kurt Bluemel, Inc., 2740 Greene Lane, Baldwin, MD 21013

Lamb Nurseries, East 101 Sharp Avenue, Spokane, WA 99202

Logee's Greenhouses, 141 North Street, Danielson, CT 06239

Park Seed, Cokesbury Road, Greenwood, SC 29647

Plant Delights Nursery, 9241 Sauls Road, Raleigh, NC 27603

Plantworld Seeds, Saint Marychurch Road, Newton Abbot, Devon TQ12 4SE, U.K.

Rocknoll Nursery, 9210 U.S. # 50 East, Hillsboro, OH 45133

Stokes' Seeds, Inc., P.O. Box 548, Buffalo, NY 14240

Swan Island Dahlias, P.O. Box 700, Canby, OH 97013

Syracuse Pottery, Inc., 6551 Pottery Road, Warners, NY 13164

Thompson & Morgan, P.O. Box 1308, Jackson, NJ 18527

W. Atlee Burpee & Co., 300 Park Avenue, Warminster, PA 18974

Woodlanders, Inc., 1128 Colleton Avenue, Aiken, SC 29801

INDEX